Centre for Baptist Studies in

Volume 24

'A Woman Shall Do It':

Edith Gates, Neglected Pioneer (1883-1962)

Christopher Voke

Regent's Park College, Oxford

Regent's Park College is a Permanent Private Hall of The University of Oxford.

Centre for Baptist Studies in Oxford
(formerly the Centre for Baptist History and Heritage)
Regent's Park College,
Pusey Street,
Oxford, OX1
2LB.
(Regent's Park College is a Permanent Private Hall of
The University of Oxford.)
www.rpc.ox.ac.uk

19 18 17 16 15 14 13   7 6 5 4 3 2 1

British Library Cataloguing in Publication Data
A catalogue record for this book is available from the British Library

ISBN: 9798387144516

Cover Illustration: Edith Gates in 1927 from the Minutes of Oxford Baptist Association,
1927. The Angus Library and Archives, Regent's Park College, Oxford.

Typeset by Larry J. Kreitzer

TABLE OF CONTENTS

Acknowledgments...vii

List of Illustrations...ix

Chapter 1: Origins...1

Chapter 2: The Move to Little Tew..13

Chapter 3: Pastor of a Village Church.......................................27

Chapter 4: The *Baptist Times* Exchange about
       'Lady Pastors'...35

Chapter 5: Formal Agreement...45

Chapter 6: Opposition and Resignation...................................47

Chapter 7: Wider Ministry..53

Chapter 8: Elizabeth Gates..59

Chapter 9 The Begnning of the End.......................................63

Chapter 10: Edith Gates' Preaching.......................................67

Chapter 11: Retirement and Final Years..................................77

Chapter 12: A Credible Ministry...81

Appendices..91

Appendix 1   *Banbury Advertiser* report of Gates' address;
              'The Attitude of Christ to the Nation'. 21 May 1931, p.5
Appendix 2   Enhanced account of 'The Attitude of Christ
              to the Nation' in the Oxfordshire and East
              Gloucestershire Baptist Association Minutes, May 19
              and 20, 1931, p. 144.ff
Appendix 3   Sermon notes in 1931 *Annual Report* of the
              Oxfordshire and East Gloucestershire Baptist Association
              (pp. 1-2).
Appendix 4   Baptist Union of Great Britain Minutes 1925-26
Appendix 5   Edith Gates' obituary

Bibliography..105

Acknowledgement

A student on the Equipped to Minister Course in Baptist History at Spurgeon's College submitted an excellent and moving essay on Edith Gates. It was creatively written using the very limited material available. So, this book is offered with thanks to Helen Culy who drew fresh attention to this remarkable woman. Many others have encouraged and supported the project. To name a few with gratitude: Emily Burgoyne and Rebecca Shuttleworth at the Angus Library; Rob Bradshaw the Spurgeon's librarian and assistant Valerie Ching; Mike Thornton and Ben Scadden at Epsom Baptist Church; Peter Mattey and Tony Woolfenden of the Belmont and South Cheam Residents' Association; Laurence Spring at the Surrey History Centre; Little Tew locals Mike Tomlinson, John Edginton, Bee and James Hayward (who live in the former Baptist chapel and School Room) and Canon William Burke; Steve Christian in Weston-Super-Mare; my sister Wendy Hofer for family research; and not least my former colleagues Pieter Lalleman and Ian Randall for much sustained encouragement, dependable help and sound advice.

CV
April 2023

List of Illustrations

Cover Illustration Edith Gates, Minutes of Oxfordshire Baptist Association, 22nd Sept 1927, p.76. Used by kind permission of the Angus Library and Archive, Regent's Park College Oxford. Colourized by Zachary Voke.

1. 1 Belmont Road, Belmont, Epsom, Surrey. The author.
2. 1 Station Road, Belmont, Epsom, Surrey, Plate 15 www.bscra.com/history.html used by permission.
3. 1 Station Road, Belmont, Epsom, Surrey. The author
4. Belmont Free Church iron chapel, Downs Road, Belmont (exterior) c. 1900. Reproduced by permission of Surrey History Centre. Copyright of Surrey History Centre.
5. Philip Marcus Ward c. 1910 Stockwell, A. H., *The Baptist Churches of Surrey* (London: Arthur H. Stockwell, ND [1909]). Facing page 17.
6. Concordance dedication. Front leaf. Used by kind permission of the Angus Library and Archive, Regent's Park College.
7. Portion of Ordnance Survey, Surrey XIX.3, 1913.
8. Baptist Manse, Little Tew, Oxfordshire. The author.
9. Philip Marcus Ward, *Bury Free Press*, Saturday 11 April 1931, p. 4.
10. The Post Office and Chapel, Little Tew, 1907. Used by permission of Oxfordshire County Council – Oxfordshire History Centre.
11. Mrs Elizabeth (Lizzie) Hughes Minutes of Oxford Baptist Association, 22nd Sept 1927, p.76. Used by kind permission of the Angus Library and Archive, Regent's Park College Oxford.
12. Little Tew and Cleveley Chapels, Oxfordshire. The author.

13. Little Tew Chapel and adjacent thatched cottage 1915. Used by permission of Oxfordshire County Council – Oxfordshire History Centre.
14. Deaconesses c. 1920, source unknown.
15. Frank J Walkey, Minutes of Oxfordshire Baptist Association, 22nd Sept 1927, p.76. Used by kind permission of the Angus Library and Archive, Regent's Park College Oxford.
16. C. V. Wilkins. Minutes of Oxfordshire Baptist Association, 22nd Sept 1927, p.76. Used by kind permission of the Angus Library and Archive, Regent's Park College Oxford.
17. Little Tew Village with chapel and converted schoolroom, 1960. Used by permission of Oxfordshire County Council – Oxfordshire History Centre.
18. Little Tew Baptist schoolroom. The author.
19. Elizabeth Gates with Edith and Frank Walkey, 1925. Used by kind permission of the Angus Library and Archive, Regent's Park College Oxford.
20. Edith Gates' retirement bungalow, Hillcote Estate, Weston-Super-Mare. The author.

Chapter 1: Origins

On a Sunday morning in February 1951 the large congregation in Clarence Park Baptist Church, Weston-Super-Mare, looked on with surprise, and some with gasps of dismay, as a tall and imposing woman in a dark suit and hat entered the pulpit to lead the service and preach. The previous Friday evening the church secretary, Ralph Hobbs, had taken a phone call from the minister, Rev. Victor Smith. He was unwell and would not be able to preach that weekend. Hobbs decided to ask a recently retired minister who had begun attending the church to step in at short notice. She answered, 'Yes, I can do that.' She appeared, without further discussion, in the pulpit on the Sunday morning. A deacons' meeting soon followed and several members had written to Hobbs firmly stating: 'We do not want women in <u>our</u> pulpit.'[1]

The Rev Edith Gates was well used to this reaction from some people in the churches where she preached and served in Oxfordshire. For thirty-two years she had been a highly honoured local church pastor, often celebrated as 'the first woman Baptist minister'. During the years of her retirement in Weston-Super-Mare Miss Gates was hardly called on to preach, or to speak at meetings in the surrounding Somerset churches. Many years before and in other contexts she had courageously faced, and convincingly overcome resistance to her public ministry as a woman. She neither needed, nor wished to fight that battle again. She was already a pioneer of women's pastoral

---

[1] Interview with Ray Green, Weston-Super-Mare, July 2020 and Green, R., *More about Christ's People at Clarence Park,* (Weston-Super-Mare: Ray Green, 2008), p. 25.

ministry in Baptist churches in the UK; the first of her kind. She enjoyed a happy and fulfilling retirement in other ways.

But who was Edith Gates? She seems to appear from nowhere. Where did she come from? What motivated her to set her course as a pioneer of women's ministry? How did she come to be pastor of a village Baptist church in rural Oxfordshire at the age of 35? What challenges did she have to overcome? These questions have never been answered. It is time to correct the neglect of this remarkable woman and tell her story in more detail.

2. Edith Gates' first home, 1 Belmont Road

Edith Gates was born on 22nd March, 1883 in Sutton, Surrey,[2] and during her childhood lived at 1, Belmont Road in the small village of Belmont a mile south of Sutton.[3] Hers was a working class family with strong aspirations for improvement. Edith later spoke of the influence of a godly father and mother'[4] and the family contacts and relationships over the years indicate that they attended church and were prayerful practising Christians. Edith's father, James Gates, had been a labourer, a greengrocer and then a 'carman', providing carting transport for local businesses. Later he created his own family coal merchants. He was able to provide well for his family and to improve their lives. By 1901 they had moved round the corner into a more spacious 5-bedroom house in Station Road, Belmont.[5] Edith's father James died in

---

[2] Aubrey, M.E., *The Baptist Who's Who: An Authoritative Reference Work and Guide to the Careers of Ministers and Lay Officials of the Baptist Churches* (London: Shaw Publ., 1934), p. 47.

[3] 1891 census of England, Surrey, Belmont, James Gates household.

[4] *Banbury Advertiser*, Oxfordshire, 21 May 1931, p. 5.

[5] 1901 census, Belmont, James Gates household.

1905, but in her widowhood Mrs Mary Gates could claim to have 'independent living and private means'.[6]

Edith had two older sisters, Florence and Annie, who had left the home before Edith was born.[7] She had an older brother George (1879-1943) who was a significant part of her life. A third sister, Elizabeth (1881-1960), two years her senior, was Edith's lifelong companion. The family of five therefore were living during all her childhood and younger years in the recently built, three-bedroomed house in Belmont Road and then at a larger house, 'Selborne', 1 Station Road, Belmont. Her brother George took over his father's coal merchant business and married Rose Truelove of Sutton in 1903, but Elizabeth and Edith declared 'private means' like their mother. They both remained single all their lives.

3/4 Edith Gates' home, 1901-1911 'Selborne', Station Road. Belmont (c. 1910 and today)

Housing and population began to expand in 19th century Belmont. It became a fruitful target for voluntary church missions. In Sutton, a mile or so away, lived a well-to-do family of musical women teachers, Mrs Eliza Hale (teacher of music) and her three daughters. Leonide Ada was a 'daily governess' and Amy and Annie were 'teachers of music'.[8] In 1878 Leonide started a Sunday School in Belmont, first in a cottage,

---

[6] 1911 census, Belmont, Mary Gates household.
[7] 1881 census, Sutton, James Gates household.
[8] 1891 census, Sutton, Eliza L. Hale household.

then as numbers grew to 100 children, in a hired barn. 'In 1889, asked to leave the barn at short notice, she managed with the help of friends to obtain land and funds to buy an iron church building for £30'.[9] Her backers were 'some gentlemen from Sutton'.[10] The building was placed on the site, now 35 Downs Road, Belmont. So, Miss Hale's Sunday School became Belmont Interdenominational Mission, with several denominations represented among the members.

Convincing evidence that it was Leonide Hale who started the Sunday School leading to the founding of the church is provided by Hilda Dancy in a letter. Her great uncle, the Belmont Station Master, Herbert John Fleetwood, married Leonide Hale in 1882.[11] In the letter Dancy recalls being told that 'Aunt Leonide had once built a tin church'. She rightly concludes that this must have been the one in Downs Road.[12]
C. H. Spurgeon took an interest in the new congregation, and it was formed into a Baptist Mission Church. Initially, services were conducted by students from the Pastor's College (now Spurgeon's College), then under the ministry of two pastors (Rev D. Henderson and Dr Neatby).[13] It was in this unassuming church, with its fast-deteriorating building, that Edith Gates was nurtured and developed as a teacher, a leader and pastor.

---

[9] Belmont and South Cheam Residents Association: www.bscra.com/History.html and edithstreets.com [accessed 9.22].

[10] Stockwell, A. H., *The Baptist Churches of Surrey* (London: Arthur H. Stockwell, ND) p. 17.

[11] 'Leonide Ada Hale' (1882), *Marriage Certificate of Herbert John Fleetwood and Leonide Ada Hale in the Parish Church of St Katherine Cree, London.* August 16th, 1882.

[12] Dancey, Miss Hilda M., letter to Mr W. Carpenter, 9th Jan. 1983; in the possession of Tony Woolfenden of Sutton.

[13] Stockwell, p. 17.

5. Belmont Interdenominational Mission chapel in Downs Road, c. 1910.
Copyright of Surrey History Centre

Philip Marcus Ward

We may now address one of our mysteries. How did a single, apparently unqualified, but aspiring working-class young woman move from a suburb in Surrey and become the highly regarded and pioneering minister of a village Baptist Church in Oxfordshire? The key is the Rev Philip Marcus Ward (1878-1931).

Philip Ward lived his early years in Sutton and Carshalton. He knew the area well. His father was of independent means, with 'income derived from houses'.[14] Philip attended Carshalton College, founded 'to provide a good education for the sons of ministers' and sons of laymen.[15] He confessed faith in Christ at a Salvation Army meeting in Portsmouth in 1902.[16] After marriage in 1904 he returned to his home area and joined Epsom Baptist Church.[17] By 1907 he appears in the

---

[14] *Census of England* 1881, Sutton, Surrey, James Ward household.

[15] *Baptist Union Handbook 1917*, p. 403.

[16] O. D. Wiles, Obituary, *BU Handbook 1932,* p. 333.

[17] *Epsom Baptist Church, minute of members meeting (extracts)*, 27 Feb. 1907, held at Epsom Baptist Church.

London and Suburban Baptist Directory list of 'Ministers without churches and occasional preachers' and is commended as a preacher by his church.[18] The Epsom members were also supportive of his early work at Belmont.[19] He was not long without a church to lead. In August of that year, he was invited to be the pastor of the Downs Road Mission, which had become Belmont Baptist Church.[20] He was 24 years old. His energy and enthusiasm soon meant he had 'a growing measure of success and encouragement'. By 1911 the church had 38 members, an expanding Sunday School, and active organisations. He led regular open-air preaching, at which he excelled and which he had started at Epsom.[21] The church secretary was the long-serving station master at Belmont, A. H. Pope.[22]

---

[18] Breed, G. ed., *The Baptist Almanack, 1886-1914, London and Suburban Baptist Directory,* (Gillingham: G.R. Breed, 2001) 1907, p. 36.

[19] *Epsom Baptist Church, minute of members meeting (extracts)*, Oct. 10, 1907.

[20] Whitley, W.T., *The Baptists of London* (London: Kingsgate Press, [N.D.]), p 296 and *Ordnance Survey*, Surrey, sheet XIX.3 (Banstead; Carshalton; Sutton and Cheam, 1913).

[21] Stockwell, pp. 17 and 18 and *Epsom Baptist Church, minute of members meeting (extracts)*, 27 Feb. 1907.

[22] *BU Handbook, 1913*, p. 120 and *UK Railway Employment Records, 1883-1956*, p. 30. A. H. Pope remained a member until his death in 1928: *Communion Register, Belmont Free Church, Interdenominational Mission*, Item 3470/2/1 held at Surrey History Centre, Woking.

6. Philip Marcus Ward c. 1910

More significant for our quest, the Gates family of Station Road were members, including two sisters in their 20s, Elizabeth and Edith Gates. Mrs Mary Gates, widowed in 1905, was involved and noted as one of the 'fellow workers at Belmont Baptist Chapel'.[23] Both her daughters played the organ, or piano and both were teaching in the lively Sunday School.[24] From 1905 the Sunday School minutes record their regular and dedicated involvement with the children of the church.[25] Edith was at first responsible for the Senior Boys Bible Class and Elizabeth the Young Women's Bible Class.[26] Edith's boys were difficult and she pleaded for her colleagues 'to bring these lads to the throne of grace in their prayers'. She persisted in her task until January 1910.[27]

Their young pastor, Philip Ward, was a 'vigorous and able preacher of the Calvin school… with a firm grip of the gospel'. He was regarded in later years as 'a preacher of conviction', but with whom 'forceful words

---

[23] *Belmont Baptist Chapel Sunday School Minute Book, 1907*, January 24, Surrey History Centre, 3470/1/1.

[24] Craig, C. Leslie, *Splendid the Heritage: the story of Belmont and its Methodist Church* (Craig, 1965).

[25] *Belmont SS Minute Book*, 1905-1911. Surrey History Centre, 3470/1/1.

[26] *Belmont SS Minute Book*, 1905, January 26 and 1906, January 8.

[27] *Belmont SS Minute Book*, 1908, September 24 and 1910, January 23.

never lacked the wooing and winsome note'.[28] He was an excellent model for the developing woman preacher sitting in his congregation, at the organ each Sunday, or at the Thursday evening preaching service, and as he chaired the Sunday School teachers' meetings. He was also 'a man of blithe and buoyant disposition which showed itself in his contact with all and sundry' [29] and 'he had a large, brotherly heart'.[30] He worked for four years in this modest, but active church, side by side with an intelligent and energetic 'sister' his own age. He knew Edith Gates well and saw her gifts and potential.

There was also a musical connection between them. Ward was known to be 'of a musical turn... as able and willing to train a choir as to conduct a Bible class or a preaching service'.[31] The piano playing founder of the church, Leonide Hale, had married Herbert Fleetwood and moved to Vancouver,[32] but her place at the piano was taken by others, including the two Miss Gates. Elizabeth was noted in later years as the organist in her sister's church.[33] Edith also played the piano and organ. At least from the age of thirteen she had served the people in worship at Belmont Baptist Chapel.

When she gave up this role, the church presented her with a *Cruden's Concordance*.[34] After her death at Weston-Super-Mare in 1962, this book was given to Ray Green by Edith Gates' pastor and executor, Rev Victor J Smith of Clarence Park Baptist Church.[35] It is inscribed on the flyleaf,

---

[28] Obituary, O. D. Wiles, *BU Handbook 1932,* p. 333.

[29] *Bury Free Press*, Saturday 11 April 1931, p. 4.

[30] Obituary, Wiles, *1932.*

[31] Obituary, Wiles, *1932.*

[32] Dancey, letter 1983.

[33] Price, Francis, *A History of Little Tew.* http://www.littletew.org.uk [accessed 9.2022].

[34] Donated by Ray Green. Lodged in The Angus Library, Regent's Park College, Oxford.

[35] Ray Green interviews, 28.7.2020 and 28.11.2021 and Green, Ray, *More about Christ's People at Clarence Park, Supplement to Centenary Church History of*

> Miss Edith Gates,
> Presented by the
> Belmont Baptist Church and congregation
> as a token of affectionate esteem
> & hearty appreciation for her
> valued service as <u>organist</u>
> for twelve years.
> > Romans XII.1
> > II Timothy II.15
> > > May 1908

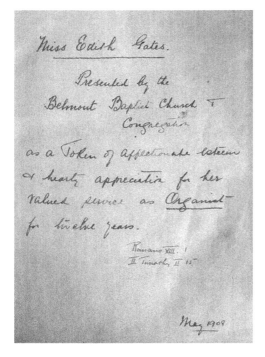

7. Concordance dedication

A further close connection existed between Ward and Edith Gates. The Wards lived in three rooms in the smaller half of 'Selbourne', Station Road, with its own front door. The house was the home of the widowed Mary Gates and her two single daughters. Ward, who lived off his property and other private income, was a lodger of Mrs Gates at seven shillings a week.[36] Ward's good influence on and close connection with Edith in all these respects is clear.

So also is the manner in which he demonstrated a way into accredited Baptist ministry. For ten years the Baptist Union had worked to arrange means by which serving ministers could be 'accredited' and consequently gain practical and financial benefits from recognition. Philip Ward was one such. He never attended a Baptist college, but in 1911 after four years ministry at Belmont he was called to pastor the twin Baptist Churches of Little Tew and Cleveley in rural Oxfordshire. Soon active in the Oxfordshire Baptist Association, he served on its General Committee with growing respect and was appointed as moderator for two churches, Chidlington and Charlebury, which were joining the Baptist Union and the Association. Then in 1914 he applied to the Association Committee, and they agreed to recommend him 'for the non-collegiate examination preliminary to recognition' as a probationer Baptist minister.[37] He duly sat and passed the required exams and in October 1915 gained the support of the Committee to be transferred to the accredited ministers' list. This commendation also included agreed money for the church at Little Tew from the newly organised Sustentation Fund.[38] He is soon listed as an accredited Baptist Minister.[39]

As we shall see, Edith Gates was close by and was watching carefully. Ward was modelling for her the 'non-collegiate' route into Baptist

---

[36] Electoral Register of Lodgers, Sutton, 1911, D. 952.

[37] *Minutes of the Oxfordshire Baptist Association Committee*, Wednesday July 8, 1914.

[38] *Minutes OBA Committee*, Wednesday October 4, 1915.

[39] *BU Handbook 1917*, p. 304.

ministry and accreditation. She was to follow exactly that same path. For a woman in an exclusive male world, it was to be, as she later expressed it, a 'startling' decision. Somehow, she stepped seamlessly into the minister's role previously occupied by Ward at Little Tew and Cleveley and became the pastor of the two churches from 1918. That is how Edith Gates got from a small town in Surrey to rural Oxfordshire.

Philip Marcus Ward made it possible.

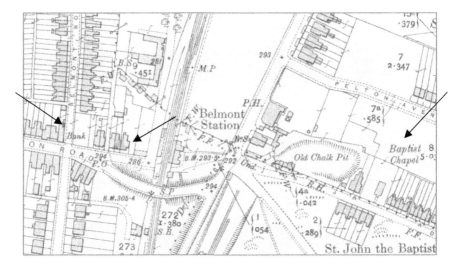

8. The map, c. 1910, shows Belmont Road and [Stati]on Road, where The Gates family lived and the 'Baptist Chapel' in Downs Road.

Chapter 2: The Move to Little Tew

However, we need to track back, since the story of Gates' ministry at Little Tew begins well before her appointment as pastor. She was already there. In 1911, when Philip and Lilly Ward moved from Belmont to Oxfordshire, their close friends Elizabeth and Edith Gates, then 30 and just turned 28, went with them.

A specially-called meeting of the Belmont Chapel Sunday School teachers took place on April 30th that year. Edith announced to the church that she and her sister were leaving. The minute reads,

> the reason of (sic) the meeting was to elect a secretary and librarian in the place of the Misses Gates, who were leaving us immediately to go to Little Tew in Oxfordshire.[1]

9. The Baptist Manse, Little Tew

With a little imagination we can reconstruct the scene: Ward was called to be minister of Little Tew. He told the sisters. They were heartbroken. He said, 'Why don't you come too?' They were delighted and began packing. All four of them moved in May 1911 and lived together in the four

---

[1] *Belmont SS Minute Book*, 1911, April 30th.

bedroomed Little Tew manse in Water Lane half a mile from the chapel. The 'Old Manse' is presently privately owned and functions as a luxury AirBnB.

Over the next seven years of Ward's ministry Edith Gates and her sister Elizabeth were deeply involved in the Little Tew Baptist Church and at the chapel in Cleveley, three and a half miles to the south. This was a most productive period for the two churches. There were effectively four 'ministers'; Philip Ward and his wife Lilly, Edith Gates and her sister Elizabeth. They were a deeply committed team, based in the church manse, and serving the two churches. Edith soon became Church Secretary and Elizabeth led the Sunday School. The annual reports of those years to the Oxfordshire Association reflect the buoyant mood of the members, with local missions, open air services in surrounding villages and growth in numbers at services. The two sisters are mentioned in connection with women's work, growth among the young people and the two Sunday Schools.[2]

10. Philip Marcus
Ward 1930

Consequently, when in 1918 Ward went to pastor the Baptist church at Milton under Wychwood, the members already had come to value Edith's gifts and observe her character. With Ward's encouragement the church invited Edith to take up his duties. At first 'Miss E. Gates' was named in the *Baptist Union Handbook* under the column for 'Church Secretary'[3] (which might be either of the sisters) but by 1924 the pastor was listed as 'Miss E Gates' who had served from 1918 and the secretary was Miss B Gates, Beth, or Betty to distinguish her from her sister. They were happily settled in the manse at Little Tew and serving the two churches. Their partnership was working

---

[2] *OBA, Annual Reports*, May 1911, p. 20, 1912, p.21, 1913, p. 22, 1916 p.21
[3] *BU Handbook 1921*, p. 90

well. Many thanks are due to Philip Marcus Ward for Edith's move to Little Tew.

11. The Post Office and Chapel, Little Tew, 1907.

A Woman Baptist Minister?

If Philip Ward was the immediate practical connection by which Gates moved to her ministry in Oxfordshire, other factors were also at play to prepare her for a pioneer role as a woman Baptist minister. She lived her younger years in the exhilarating context of the battle for women's suffrage. There is no clear evidence that she was an activist or involved politically, but it is impossible to imagine that the influential women of her exact age did not profoundly impact the view she had of herself and her future. The Suffragette leader Emmeline Pankhurst (1858-1928) had two daughters, Christabel (1880-1958) and Sylvia (1882-1960). They were Gates' precise contemporaries, visible and active in the struggle for woman's liberation and suffrage. The Suffragette Emily Wilding Davison, a little older (1872-1913), died in a tragic publicity stunt at Epsom racecourse, not four miles distant from the Gates' home at Belmont.

Many more of her exact contemporaries were active in the Suffragist movement. In addition, many influential men supported the cause from principle, among whom was a notable Baptist minister, Dr John Clifford, pastor of a large and very influential London Baptist church, Westbourne Park in Paddington. Of wide and radical sympathy, Clifford was for many years a vice-president of the London Society for Women's Suffrage, fighting for women's suffrage and equality.[4] It is hardly possible that Edith Gates was ignorant of such influences. Her subsequent determination to seek accreditation as a Baptist minister demonstrates the powerful effect of the women's suffrage movement and the accompanying struggle for women's equality and freedom.

Many other women, growing up in this atmosphere and beyond the politics of the suffragists, were taking up church roles previously occupied only by men. The Church League for Women's Suffrage was founded in 1909 and the corresponding and more militant Free Church League for Women's Suffrage in 1910. Edith Gates' call to Christian

---

[4] e.g., the *London Society for Women's Suffrage Annual Report, 1912*, p. 5.

ministry and the opportunity that she took to respond may be placed at exactly this moment.

Another woman who responded to the same call to ministry was Margaret Fullerton, neé Hardy (1891-1980), who subsequently became one of the first ordained woman Congregational ministers.[5] As a child Hardy attended a Plymouth Brethren Assembly and so, exactly like Edith Gates, was formed as a Christian in a small independent and conservative evangelical church. However, on arriving in London in 1908 to study as a young woman aged 17, she met and came under the exciting influence of the famous suffragist leaders. She worked for a while in the office of the National Union of Women's Suffrage Societies and was exposed not only to the political message of women's suffrage, but also to the speeches of deeply committed Christian suffragists. One of these was Maud Royden, who was advocating equality in church ministry and was instrumental in the founding of the Church League for Women's Suffrage.

The profound influence of all this on young Christian women is illustrated by the report of a conversation, when after hearing an address by Maud Royden in 1917, Margaret Hardy conveyed her appreciation, saying,

> You know, do you not, that there is an ever-increasing number of young women, enthusiastic and full of hope, 'ready for anything', who are willing to follow Maude Royden wherever she may lead ...?[6]

Sylvia Dunkley comments, 'as did many women'.[7]

---

[5] Dunkley, Sylvia, *Women Magistrates, Ministers and Municipal Councillors in the West-Riding of Yorkshire, 1918 – 1939* (Submitted for the Degree of Doctor of Philosophy, Department of History, University of Sheffield, August 1991) pp. 268-279.

[6] *Maude Royden Papers*, Letter to Maude Royden from Margaret Hardy, 21st March 1917 quoted in Dunkley p. 270.

[7] Dunkley, p. 270.

We must place Edith Gates exactly in the context of this powerful movement. There is one piece of evidence which points to Gates' involvement with the suffragists. In Beckenham, on Saturday, September 24th 1910, *A Pageant of Great Women* written by Cicely Hamilton was performed twice.[8] It was one of a series of events associated with the developing moves towards woman's suffrage, freedom and equality. In dramatic form the pageant presented great women of world history. It involved a cast of at least 60, mainly young women. The advertisement called on supporters to 'proclaim your pride in womanhood' and for every woman present to thank God that she belongs to the sex that, in spite of fearful odds, has left such a splendid record upon the annals of history.'[9] The script did not specifically mention suffrage, it was written to oppose prejudice and to stress the urgent need for equality and freedom for women. However, a report on the event noted that 'the representation is a powerful argument for giving women the vote'. The drama clearly opposed 'the contention of prejudice that woman is not fit for freedom'. The writer continued,

> There pass in the pageant, at the call of Woman pleading to Justice for the "clear right to call my life my own", groups of women who were learned, women who were saintly, women who fought as bravely as men when need arose, women who against great odds achieved distinction...

The villain 'Prejudice', a man opposed to women's political freedom, eventually gave up and slinked off the stage. The enthusiastic report concluded:

> The pageant is a forcible argument in favour of women's equality with men, and we heard on Saturday many expressions of opinion that it would enormously advance women's cause.

And what has this to do with Edith Gates? The participants listed were largely single women in their twenties and thirties. Some were

---

[8] Hamilton, C., *A Pageant of Great Women* (London: The Suffrage Shop, 1910)
[9] *The Vote*, Saturday, September 10, 1910, p. 231.

suffragist activists and some their female relatives.[10] The Beckenham Journal had carried advertisements appealing for 'ladies who are willing to take part'. The advert stressed there was 'no speaking required', the actors merely appeared on stage one by one. Applicants were only asked to send in their names if they wished to participate.[11] At the top of the list of actors for the numerous parts we read:

'The following took roles: - Hypatia, Edith Gates.'[12]

It is impossible without clearer evidence to establish with certainty the identity of this Edith Gates. It was not a unique name at the time, but in Southeast London it was. We know of her later skills as a very effective communicator and of her 'imposing' persona, so it can be fairly concluded that here is our Edith Gates. She would have been 27 years old, single, and in 1910 still living in Belmont within easy distance of the venue. Contact with the young women in the pageant and the associated leaders of the campaign for equality cannot but have been life changing for Edith. Even if it was not her playing the part of Hypatia in this pageant, such an event clearly displays the social and political atmosphere in which movement towards equality and accreditation as a Baptist minister was, at exactly this moment, being nurtured in Edith Gates.

---

[10] e.g., Mrs Charlotte Despard and the three daughters of Mrs Kate Glanville-Harvey.

[11] *Beckenham Journal,* 30th July 1910, p. 5.

[12] *Norwood News*, Saturday, 1 October 1910, p. 4. Hypatia of Alexandria, an Egyptian mathematician and philosopher (d. 415 AD).

Contact with another woman, in the nearer orbit of Gates' early years in Oxfordshire, was with Mrs Elizabeth Hughes (1862-1946). Lizzie Hughes was the daughter of George Cooper, baker and confectioner of Oxford, and Mayor in 1895-96. Lizzie and her brother George H. Cooper were members of the large and influential New Road Baptist Church.[13] She had been widowed early and devoted herself to a local

mission set up by New Road in St Thomas, Oxford, at the time a deprived area of the town. She described herself as a 'Christian suffragist'. She was elected as one of the first female town Councillors and was active for many years in Liberal politics.

As an example of a woman church leader and pastor there are many connections to Gates. Hughes was titled the 'superintendent', effectively the minister, of the St Thomas mission, a post she held for 58 years.[14] She took her stand with men reporting on the varied mission activities of the New Road church.[15] In 1920 she was elected as the first woman to be the president of the Oxfordshire Baptist Association.[16] Hughes was high profile and greatly respected. She lived and worked less than twenty miles away from Little Tew. Within easy reach, here was a model for Edith Gates' own ministry of a

12. Mrs Elizabeth
Hughes in 1928

---

[13] New Road Baptist Church, *Church Book* Membership List, January 1913, p. 1.

[14] New Road Baptist Church, *Church Book*, March 2, 1910, November 1, 1911 and June 3, 1914, etc. and Chadwick, Rosie (Ed) *A Protestant Catholic Church of Christ; Essays on the history and life of New Road Baptist Church Oxford* (Oxford: New Road Baptist Church, 2003) p. 191.

[15] *The Oxford and District Free Church Magazine*, October 1907, vol. XI, no.130, p. 40.

[16] *BU Handbook*, 1921, p. 34. Her brother George Cooper was to be president in 1934.

woman leader and pastor. They were very well known to each other. Their names appear regularly, and for over 25 years, as fellow members of the General Committee of the Oxfordshire Baptist Association. They also worked together to found and lead the local branch of the Women's Prayer Circle. Only six months before her death, Lizzie Hughes was present at the celebration of twenty-eight years of Gates' ministry at Little Tew and Cleveley, when she spoke to commend Edith and her sister Elizabeth for their long and widely influential ministry.[17]

Significant shifts in thinking were taking place among the leaders of the Baptist Union, making it possible for individual women to present themselves as local church pastors and candidates for accredited Baptist ministry. At that time there were three who did so; Edith Gates was one, the others, emerging soon after, were Maria Living-Taylor and Violet Hedger. However, the possibility of appointing and accrediting a woman as minister of a Baptist church had not been formally addressed. It had hardly been mentioned as an issue. The appearance of Edith and her two fellow travelers precipitated the Baptist Union into debate about the accredited pastoral ministry of women. Their names appear in the records of the denomination, at first without debate, although as we shall see, early on there was strong resistance from some. The denomination was 'startled' into action when these women presented themselves. Each of them combined a high level of gift and a strong sense of calling together with the robust personality sufficient to face the challenge of an often-hostile context.

As it turned out these women also embodied the three possible routes and the three rules by which women (and indeed men) have applied for entry to the probationers' list over the last 100 years. Entry to this list and subsequent accreditation are precisely illustrated by the women who were just then applying to be ministers. In 1907 the Baptist Union agreed a basic set of rules for the ministerial recognition of a candidate.[18] These were significantly expanded in 1911, then further

---

[17] *Banbury Guardian*, 16 May 1946, p 3.
[18] *BU Minute Book,* 14 May 1907.

adjusted in 1919 and 1923.[19] The clauses were phrased without any thought that the candidate might be a woman. They specified for a candidate three ways that 'he' may seek to be placed on the probationers' list.[20] The timing of this ongoing discussion could not have been more significant or helpful for Edith Gates. She fits exactly into this context.

Violet Hedger (1900-1992)

Violet Maud Hedger represented 'Rule I.1', which stated that the candidate must have 'completed a course of ministerial training of not less than three years duration in one of the recognised Baptist Colleges', followed by an exam.[21] Violet was born on 5th January 1900 in Horsham, Sussex.[22] She was strong in body as well as in character. In Hornsey High School for Girls she won medals for athletics, becoming games captain and head prefect.[23] The family attended Ferme Park Baptist Church in Hornsey where the pastor was Dr Charles Brown (1855-1924), a highly honoured Baptist statesman known later as 'the Baptist archbishop'.[24] He built the church into a congregation of over one thousand through energetic pastoral care and evangelical preaching. The young Violet was deeply engaged in this vibrant church, and she was led to faith in Christ and baptised by Brown.

As required, she was commended for Baptist ministry by her church in June 1919. After interview and examination, the following September she entered Regent's Park College (then located in London) aged 19. She thereby became the first woman to be trained for ministry at a Baptist College. Against some severe opposition within and beyond the College, Hedger gained her BD in 1923 and was enrolled as a

---

[19] Sparkes, Douglas C., *An Accredited Ministry* (Didcot: Baptist Historical Society, 1996), pp. 25-26.

[20] Report on Ministerial Recognition, *BU Handbook, 1913,* pp. 212-213.

[21] Report, *BHB, 1913,* pp. 212f.

[22] *GRO 1900* M Quarter in Horsham, Vol. 02B, p. 310.

[23] Lewis, Vivian, *BU Handbook*, 1982, Obituary, p. 327.

[24] *Eastbourne Gazette*, Wednesday 26 June 1940, p. 5.

probationer in 1924, subsequently appearing in the published probationers list - with the men.[25] After delay and disappointment she was called to her first church in 1926 and was accredited by the Baptist Union in October 1928.[26] She pursued a courageous and effective ministry in four churches and in wider service over a long career.[27]

Maria Living-Taylor (1889-1984)

The path of Maria Living-Taylor into accredited Baptist ministry was eased because she was married to a Baptist minister, John Taylor. He had been trained as an evangelist with the Seventh Day Adventist Church and he entered the accredited list by passing the Baptist Union exams. Maria represented the second pathway into accreditation, based on the second Baptist Union rule, which stated that the candidate should have 'an adequate collegiate or university training elsewhere than in a Baptist College' and must have been working in a pastoral position for at least two years. (Rule I, 2).[28] Living-Taylor had studied at the University of Dijon and later attended East London University. In 1916 she gained a London University BA Honours degree as an external student.[29] She worked, at least from 1920, as a pastor alongside her husband and was 'enrolled' as a probationer minister in 1922. This decision was 'not without agitation' on the part of some, who saw it as the thin end of the wedge.[30] She appeared in the published list of probationers in 1924 (with the men) and was transferred to the

---

[25] *BU Handbook*, 1925, p. 235.

[26] *BU Minute Book,* Ministerial Recognition Committee, 18th October 1928, p. 414.

[27] A full account of Violet Hedger's life and early ministry may be found in Sylvia Dunkley, *Women Magistrates* (1991). See note 45.

[28] Report, *BHB, 1913,* pp. 212f.

[29] archives.libraries.london.ac.uk/resources/graduates2ocr.pdf, p. 570 [accessed 24.9.22].

[30] Northcroft, D. M., *Free Church Women Ministers* (London: Edgar G. Dunstan, 1930) p 16.

ministerial list in that year.[31] Subsequently, in her own right, jointly with her husband until 1939, she ministered in each of their five churches until together they entered educational work after 1942.[32]

Edith Gates (1883-1962)

The third path is that taken by Edith Gates. Rule I, 3 made room for her and many like her, both men and women, to be placed on the Probationers' List. It applied to,

> Pastors who have not received a training such as is described
> in Rule I, 1 and 2, but who, in the judgement of the Council,
> have efficiently exercised the office of pastor for a period of
> not less than two years.[33]

We shall see later that Gates had certainly done that. As required, she also had the recommendation of the Committees of her Baptist Association and was therefore enrolled as a probationer minister in 1922.[34] In 1927 there appeared a newly created, separate list, the 'Women Pastors'. This consisted of the two women still marked as probationers, Miss Gates and Miss Hedger and the now accredited Mrs Living-Taylor.

Each of these women was a 'first' of their kind. Maria Living-Taylor was the first woman to be enrolled as a probationer on the grounds of previous higher education and two years' pastoral service. She was then the first woman to become a fully accredited Baptist Minister (1924). Violet Hedger was the first woman to train at a Baptist College and be accredited (1928). Edith Gates was the first woman called to pastor a Baptist church (1918) and subsequently to be accredited (1929). They were all pioneers in contrasting ways, demonstrating different routes into accredited ministry. Each won formal approval locally and

---

[31] *BU Minute Book,* Ministerial Recognition Committee, 17th November 1924, p. 515.

[32] *BU Handbook,* 1941, pp. 255 and 283.

[33] Report on Ministerial Recognition, *BU Handbook, 1913,* pp. 212-213.

[34] *BU Minute Book,* Ministerial Recognition Committee, 7 November 1922, p. 78.

nationally and advanced significantly the acceptance of women's ordained ministry in the Baptist Union.

Chapter 3: Pastor of a Village Church

13. Little Tew and Cleveley Baptist Chapels in 2022.

The name of Edith Gates therefore appeared in the published list of probationer ministers in the Baptist Union Handbook of 1923 – with the men. Then, from 1927 in a separate list of 'Women Pastors', as a probationer minister. Having satisfied all requirements, she was accredited as a minister in 1929.[1] Her early educational background is unclear, but it was probably sparce. Free compulsory elementary education began in 1891 when she would already have been eight years old. The first 'board school' in Belmont (Cotswold Road) did not open until 1896 and a second (Avenue Road) in 1902.[2] The seven years of

---

[1] *BU Minute Book,* Ministerial Recognition Committee, 18th June 1929, p. 32.
[2] Sparkes, *Belmont: A Century Ago,* p. 9.

study she apparently needed to prepare for her exam and satisfy the
Baptist Union can be seen in the light of this background, to say nothing
of the demands of her lively church.

The story now moves to Oxfordshire and the arrival of Edith and her
sister, with Philip Marcus Ward and his wife (Lily?) in Little Tew. The
small village had been a hotbed of nonconformity from the 17th century,
with Quakers prominent for 100 years and half the population taking
the 'protestation oath' in 1642.[3] Nearby Great Tew reported 'many
Baptists' in 1834. In 1854 'the vicar said that a third of the villagers were
Baptists, or Ranters'.[4] The first vicar of Little Tew, Charles Garrett
(from 1858), was deeply opposed to nonconformity in the parish and is
reputed to have paid several Baptists to emigrate to Canada.[5]

There was a deep and vibrant tradition of dissenting families, many of
them Baptist, in the nearby villages and this led to the forming of Little
Tew Baptist church in 1778[6] when Edmund Drake 'registered his house
for dissenting meetings and taught ten Anabaptists there'.[7] Another
house was converted as a meeting room in 1829. John Hiorns applied
for 'registration of a certain building, now fitted out as a chapel, which
is intended to be used as a place of religious worship by an Assembly
or Congregation of Protestant Dissenters of the Baptist denomination'.[8]
Eight leading members of the village signed the application. Then about
1845 a Baptist chapel was built facing Water Lane which 'attracted

---

[3] A P Baggs, Christina Colvin, H M Colvin, Janet Cooper, C J Day, Nesta
Selwyn and A Tomkinson, 'Parishes: Great Tew', in *A History of the County of
Oxford: Volume 11, Wootton Hundred (Northern Part)*, ed. Alan Crossley (London,
1983), pp. 223-247. *British History Online* www.british-history.ac.uk/vch/oxon/
vol11/pp223-247 [accessed 8.22].

[4] *British History Online*, Bodlian MS. Oxf. Dioc. b 39; *Wilb. Visit.* 1501 and Baggs
et al.

[5] Price, Francis; www.littletew.org.uk [accessed 21.8.20].

[6] *BU Handbook 1913*, p. 109.

[7] *British History Online*, Bodlian MS. Oxf. Dioc. b 37, f. 102; O.R.O., Cal. Q.
Sess. viii. 809.

[8] Price, Francis.

congregations of *c*. 100 from the area around'.[9] The present building, now a private house, was opened in 1871.

14. Little Tew Post Office, Chapel and adjacent thatched cottage 1915.

As we have seen, the Gates sisters moved to the village in 1911 with the Wards and began to play an active part in the leadership and pastoral care of the twin Baptist churches. In 1912 it was reported by the church that,

> A Bible class for young women is held at the manse every Sunday afternoon, conducted by Miss Gates. A women's social is held every Wednesday afternoon at Cleveley, conducted by the Misses Gates, the attendance is exceedingly good. [10]

---

[9] *British History Online, P. O. D., Oxon.* (1847/8); P.R.O., HO 129/5/162.
[10] *OBA, 110th Annual Report*, May 1912, p. 21.

Both sisters became church members and among their many duties they acted as 'Messengers', or representatives of the church.[11] There was no question of a return to Belmont. Edith and Elizabeth were giving themselves eagerly and with considerable success to supporting Philip Ward in the leadership and pastoral care of the church and they continued to be active in the years up to 1918. In June 1917 Edith was present at the Little Tew Sunday School anniversary where, it being wartime, they collected gifts for 'midsummer parcels' to be sent to 'all the "boys" who had joined up and were in several parts of the world'. The report noted that 'Miss Edith Gates, Little Tew, is acting as secretary to the same', probably meaning she was secretary of the Sunday School.[12] In October 1918 a 'Harvest Home' was held at the sister church in Cleveley, three and a half miles to the south, with 'good congregations' and 'presided over by Miss Edith Gates'. At Little Tew later in that week they had 'a record congregation at all services'.[13]

This 'Harvest Home' celebration was six months after Philip Marcus Ward moved to Milton under Wychwood. He left the twin churches flourishing, Edith Gates was pastor in charge, her sister supporting and running a lively Sunday School. In these brief local reports, we have the first accounts of Gates' ministry and signs of her later impact. She was not yet publicly acknowledged as, or claiming to be the 'pastor', but by 1918 she is taking leadership responsibility. She quickly took up her office as pastor of the two churches — on the departure of Philip Ward.

Probationer Minister

An Oxfordshire Baptist Association Committee minute of October 1919 reads,

> The Revd C. J. Byford reported that the church at Little Tew had asked Miss Gates to continue in charge of the church until

---

[11] *OBA, 114th Annual Report*, May 1916.
[12] *Banbury Guardian,* Thursday, 21 June 1917, p. 8.
[13] *Oxfordshire Weekly News*, Wednesday, 16 Oct 1918, p. 3.

September 1920. This was approved by the Committee, and it was agreed to suggest that they allow the Misses Gates to live for this period in the manse on payment of a peppercorn rent of 10/- only. The Revd C Hobbs was asked to act as moderator of the Church.[14]

Two years later at the Oxfordshire Committee of 12th April 1921,
> The secretary reported that... Miss Gates had been formally elected to the pastorate of Little Tew and the committee supported her application to sit for the Baptist Union examination.[15]

The need for a rental agreement over the occupation of the Little Tew manse points to an added motivation for Edith Gates' decision to seek fully ordained Baptist ministry. It is a very human one. The original endowment for the building of the Little Tew chapel was made by a substantial local farmer Robert Ryman in 1871. He insisted that his tenants attended the chapel. Then in his will he provided a site for a house and income for the 'benefit of the recognised Minister or Pastor for the time being of the Protestant dissenters of the Baptist Denomination'.[16] Therefore, if Edith had not been 'ordained' then on the departure of Philip Ward she and her sister would risk losing their home. Her opponents no doubt made this point. The domestic security and the delightful surroundings, as well as Edith's continuing ministry, depended on her entering the accreditation process and being 'recognised' by the Baptist Union.

There is no existing record of an Ordination or Induction service at Little Tew for Edith Gates. We must assume that at some point such a service took place. Nonetheless, as these minutes demonstrate, the church members knew her value and affirmed her ministry in 1918. Then subsequently she was 'formally elected to the pastorate' by the

---

[14] *Minutes of the OBA Committee*, 16th October, 1919.
[15] *Minutes OBA*, 12th April 1921.
[16] wills.oxfordshirefhs.org.uk/az/wtext/ryman_033.html [Accessed April 2023].

members. Of course, the church obtained two for the price of one; Elizabeth, the irreplaceable lifelong companion, was adding her own significant value. She lived in the manse with her sister Edith and shared the burden of pastoral and leadership duties, including locally remembered duties as organist. We will return to Elizabeth later.

In these years Gates was studying in preparation for the required Baptist Union Examinations. She sat and passed the first exam in September 1922.[17] This was a significant achievement. Over this period, each year dozens of men, who like Edith had not been to a Baptist College, were seeking entry to the Probationers' List of ministers and sitting the required exams. The pass mark was 50%. The attrition rate was high. The following year's report on the results of the first exam shows that of 27 who sat, 5 passed, 3 were referred and 19 failed![18] The sad conclusion of the national Ministerial Recognition Committee was that 'the scholarship standard of the non-collegiate candidates is on the whole very low,' leading to 'appalling results in the examinations'. They drew attention to 'repeated failure' by the candidates.[19] The exam was a fearful barrier to applicants, but Edith Gates overcame it and demonstrated her application and ability.

The National MRC of 1922 noted that 'Edith Gates had settled at Little Tew and Cleveley' and that since she had fulfilled the conditions she should be enrolled on the Probationers' List.'[20] She had been commended to the Baptist Union by the Oxfordshire Baptist Association, she had just taken and successfully passed the first required examination on the 19th and 20th September 1922 and so enters the list of probationer Baptist ministers as published in the BU handbook.[21]

---

[17] *BU Minute Book,* Ministerial Recognition Committee, 7th Nov. 1922, p. 85.

[18] *BU Minute Book,* MRC Special Committee, 17th October 1923, pp. 600-602.

[19] *BU Minute Book,* MRC, 28th June 1926, p. 278.

[20] *BU Minute Book,* MRC, 7th November 1922, p. 85.

[21] *BU Handbook* 1924, p. 260.

The first group of Deaconesses training at Havelock Hall - 1920

15. This 1920 photo may include Edith Gates (left).

However, the Committee required that she pursue 'a course of training at Havelock Hall'. This was the new Deaconess Training College in Hampstead, which had opened in October 1920. The Superintendent of the Central Association, F. J. Walkey organised Edith's admission.[22] Frank Walkey was to become Gates' strong supporter over the tangled years of her progress to accredited ministry.

In case there was any resistance locally (and as we shall see, there was), six months later the Oxfordshire Association Committee confirmed their previous action 'in recommending Miss Gates to this list'.[23] Three women were present at that Committee meeting, including Lizzie Hughes. So too was Frank Walkey.

---

[22] *BU Minute Book,* 7th November 1922, p. 85.
[23] *Minutes OBA*, 1st May 1923.

Gates dutifully applied to Havelock Hall.[24] However, there is no indication that she in fact attended the College. No further mention of her 'course of training' appears in the record. (The photo above from 1920 may include Edith Gates on the left. The reader may judge.) The annual report to the Women's Committee of the BU from the efficient College Principal, Miss J. J. Arthur MA in 1924, accurately names all nine students in attendance that year, but none of them is Edith Gates. Unless she is one of the 'three outside students' mentioned, it is unlikely that she attended many lectures, if at all. She was leading a busy church. In any case she was given special consideration. The national MRC

granted her exemption from the second exam under certain conditions. They proposed that Ronald Hobling, the well-established pastor of New Road Oxford, 'be requested to provide a course of reading as an equivalent to the Second Examination, the course to be spread over a period of two years.' Ultimately the Committee offered an extension of the probationary period to give her time to complete these studies. And the committee pressed her to do so.'[25]

16. Frank Walkey in 1928

---

[24] *BU Minute Book,* Baptist Women's Training College and Sisterhood Committee, 15th January 1923, p. 213.

[25] *BU Minute Book,* MRC, November 1926, Special Cases, p. 585. *Pace* Randall, Ian, *The English Baptists of the 20th Century* (Didcot: Baptist Historical Society, 2005), p. 142.

Chapter 4: The Baptist Times Exchange
about 'Lady Pastors'

A series of letters and articles began in the *Baptist Times* in 1922. The matter of women ministers was being mentioned. It was related to the reconsideration of the way by which non-collegiate 'men' who applied for accreditation were to be assisted, if they were to be allowed to apply at all.[1] The use of the Sustentation Fund, now regularly dispersed to ministers, was also being considered. Some argued for an age limit to be applied to ministry applicants.[2] Hidden in this debate were other questions. What about non-collegiate women? Would women ministers be proper candidates for the Funds? Should financial help be only for single women ministers? The *Baptist Union Assembly* of May 1922 debated the revised rules of ministerial recognition, with special reference to non-collegiate men.[3] Consequently correspondents and contributors to the *Baptist Times*, seeing these matters reported, began to pick up the way in which the issues applied to women.

Mrs C.S. (Katherine M) Rose, the influential Organising Secretary of the Baptist Women's League, took up her formidable pen on the subject of women ministers in her weekly column. [4] She argued that since the 'transitional period between war and peace' was coming to an end, women should not try and hold on to the 'abnormal'. She stated her

---

[1] *Baptist Times and Freeman*, 7 April 1922, p. 211 and 28 April 1922, p. 264.
[2] *BT,* 16 June 1922, p. 388.
[3] *BT*, 12 May 1922, pp. 304ff.
[4] *BT*, 29 December 1922, p. 858.

view that 'wild schemes' which were neither 'practical nor natural' were impossible because they were a 'violation of the fundamental principles of natural law'. She proposes that woman's power would always lie in the realm of the 'humanitarian and spiritual not the abnormal or the secular'. About the place of women in the church (without naming her) Rose quoted the case of Violet Hedger. She pointed out that 'the woman' had been college trained and prepared, but because she was a woman, she had not received a call to a pastorate. Her main point was that since the pastoral role was closed, women must be 'guided into other channels'. There are other ways a woman can serve, she argued, in homes and in the street and notably through the sisterhood of Deaconesses, the Baptist Women's League and special services for women at Association and Union events. She seemed unaware of the woman pastor at Little Tew, or chose to ignore her.

In her final paragraph Rose hoped that 'the place of women in the Baptist world' will be settled at the forthcoming World Baptist Congress in Stockholm, with special meetings for women. In fact, she concludes, 'we might even say that it is already settled.'

She was greatly mistaken. It is not hard to imagine what effect such words had on those who took a different view. Notably on Edith Gates personally and on her supporters. Edith is being characterised as 'abnormal,' her ordination 'a wild scheme' and her ministry 'unnatural'. The swift and terse response of her church leads to a significant moment in this correspondence and in the story of women's ministry - it is a moment focused on Edith Gates. And it emerges from a humanly insignificant rural Baptist local church.

A month after the publication of the article by Rose, a brief and polite letter appeared in the *Baptist Times* correspondence section headed 'Lady Pastors'.

Lady Pastors

Sir, - Having seen in *The Daily Chronicle* of the 11th inst. That a Baptist Church in Wales has a lady pastor, we should like to say that our pastor is also a lady, Miss Edith Gates, and has held this position for the past five years, having two churches in her charge, Little Tew and Cleveley (Baptist), with a distance of four miles between each.

We had eleven members received in one year, which testifies to the good work being done. She has recently passed the BU exam, and her name enrolled upon the probationers list.

EDWARD WEBB, GEORGE DEAN,
Deacons.
Little Tew, Enstone, Oxon.[5]

The 'lady pastor' in Wales referred to by Webb and Dean in this letter was Annie Davies Lodwick. In January 1923 she had just been invited to the pastorate of Pisgah Baptist Church in Cresswell Quay, Pembrokeshire.[6] From the middle of the 19th century Welsh Baptist churches had a tradition of women 'lay preachers', which naturally created some controversy. They were titled 'Assistants', 'Helpers' or 'Auxiliary Preachers' and the number grew in the early 20th century so that some gained recognition as 'preachers' from the Welsh Baptist Associations. It was in 1923 that Lodwick was ordained in Pisgah, 'a significant church with 119 members', and so became the first recognised Baptist minister in Wales. Health concerns and continuing resistance in the churches to the idea of women ministers meant she was not consistently able to serve as a pastor, but she had a wide evangelistic and preaching ministry.[7]

---

[5] *BT,* 19 January 1923, p. 41.

[6] www.pisgah.org.uk/annie-lodwock.

[7] Collis, Michael J. (2014) Female Baptist Preachers and Ministers in Wales, *BQ,* 45:8, 465-484.

The letter from these Little Tew deacons breathes pride in their 'lady pastor' by the church and reflects fair courage to speak up for her in the context of this debate and not to let her be overlooked. It would be surprising if Edith herself were not party to the exact wording of it. It is full of important insights, albeit brief and modest in content. It works out a clear Baptist ecclesiology in a simple local context.

First, it contains the essence of what Baptist ministry is; the minister is attached to one specific church, in two congregations in this case, Little Tew and Cleveley.

Second, she has the pastoral 'charge' of this church, so her position as pastor has implicit local responsibilities of ruling, teaching and pastoral care.

Third, the deacons and members consider her 'our pastor'. They have appointed her and so they in turn have responsibilities towards her of care, material support and cooperation.

Fourth, the evidence of a valid and settled ministry is the 'good work' being done. The two deacons on behalf of the members testify to the blessing of God upon it through the application of her spiritual gifts.

Fifth, the church and their pastor do not act alone, but look for affirmation and recognition from the wider church for their pastor's ministry. In this case it is through connection with the Oxfordshire Baptist Association and the Baptist Union using the processes of probationary enrolment, including the first 'BU exam', and the subsequent ministry accreditation as a probationer which by this time in 1923 was in place.

Sixth, and this is the main point of the letter; no matter what anyone argues, Edith Gates is presently the duly appointed and serving woman pastor of this Baptist Church. She has been in this position, into which all the members placed her, 'for five years'. We know from other evidence that she was appointed by vote of the members going back to 1918. The church regarded that decision as the start of her ministry.

The mutual commitment expressed, and the strength of the bond between pastor and people reflected in this letter demonstrate the power of Baptist church polity from the earliest days. A church is essentially a covenanted community, congregationally ruled, and responsibly led. In Little Tew the church is properly ordered and effectively served by a woman minister, Edith Gates.

It is worth pausing to note that the whole ethos of Baptist life, its congregational polity and the methods of procedure are vividly illustrated by the events leading to this letter. It shows that the mood in Baptist churches was changing in response to new views about women's freedom and equality in society. A few courageous local churches were adapting their views and were willing to act accordingly. They convinced leading men and women of some associations and colleges. The councils of the denomination had then to respond and engage in a more thorough debate. In other words, the ground-breaking change came not from wide theological consideration or denominational initiative. It came from a small local church and from unknown individuals who were willing to follow what they knew to be the call of God on their lives. The accreditation and ordination of women into the Baptist ministry emerged from below. This process was a faithful reflection of the way that the original Baptist churches formed in the 17th century; by fearless individuals and groups of committed supporters acting in response to their call, in accord with their conscience, and ordering themselves communally with others of like mind.

Reaction to the information in the Little Tew letter was immediate. One anonymous correspondent simply asked,

Is there any scriptural authority for women ministers in view of 1 Cor. xvi. 34 and 35 and 1 Tim. ii. 11 and 12? J.D.M.

Katherine M Rose (Mrs C S Rose of the previous article) replied to
'J.D.M.' in an ambiguous letter. She maintained that preaching and
prophesying in the New Testament are the same and that women
therefore may preach. Then, strangely in view of her previous
statements, said,

> It would, at least, be as difficult to prove, from the passages
> quoted by your correspondent, that women are forbidden to
> act as pastors as it would be to prove that the modern pastor
> performs the same function as his predecessors in the New
> Testament.[8]

The two contributions from Mrs Rose seem contradictory. However,
her view that women should be excluded from pulpit and pastoral
charge was based not on 'the passages quoted', but were expressed as
an expedient; simply that ordained women pastors were not acceptable
to the churches. She hinted at this view in her earlier article, where her
plea for strengthened special women's activity in the churches was
because 'the pulpit may not be open to her at the present'. But to
churches like Little Tew the pulpit was already open.

The debate on 'Women as Pastors' continued in further letters. Harry
Preece of Ramsgate, a retired Baptist Minister, stressed that although
according to the New Testament women may be deacons, there is not

> any instance of a woman being set apart to the overseership,
> or acting in that capacity; neither is there any suggestion of
> an open door in that direction.[9]

Derek Bedford, a young man at a Public School, was interested in the
questions of 'J.D.M.', but took 'a saner view'; 'if a woman knows that
she is called of God to minister for him, she should become a minister.
Why would God call else?'[10]

---

[8] *BT,* 2 February 1923, p. 80
[9] *BT,* 9 February 1923, p. 40
[10] *BT,* 16 February 1923, p. 116

In a questioning letter, W T Reynolds of Bishop Stortford wrote on behalf of others in the denomination,

> many of us still remain convinced that the appointment of lady pastors is a grave departure from scriptural order, a pandering to the modern blight of lawlessness, and a thing to be deplored. One is startled to read that the Baptist Union is to recognise women as accredited ministers. Has this unscriptural innovation really been accepted by the assembly?[11]

A Presbyterian, Mackenzie Bell, entered the discussion, concluding about St Paul's ban that he 'was laying down, with the discernment of supreme genius a wise temporary rule.'

Finally, the editor drew the discussion to an end, stating,

> we have received other letters on this subject, for which we regret we cannot find room. This correspondence must now close, but we will ask a recognised theologian to sum up the correspondence and state the theological position.[12]

No summing up by a theologian appeared. The only response at this crucial point seems to have been the 1923 Presidential Address by W E Blomfield on 23rd April at the Baptist Assembly. It was entitled 'The Ministry and the Churches'. In this extensive address he makes no mention of women at all. The second heading reads 'We must take our Share in the Calling of Men to the Ministry'. The language is consistently framed in the masculine, so that for our ministry we need 'men of the best type'. If this were considered a response to the concerns of the letter writers, or the denomination, it is woefully inadequate. Today it would be ruled offensive.[13]

---

[11] *BT,* 16 February 1923, p. 116.
[12] *BT,* 23 February 1923, p. 133.
[13] *BT,* 27 April 1923, pp. 299ff.

In fact, events had entirely overtaken the denomination. Reynolds in his letter (above) tells us he was 'startled'. This is a term that Edith Gates takes up in at least one public address. She is not afraid to 'startle' the denomination. She and her little church, along with her two ministry women travellers, had already done so. It was agreed locally; 'our pastor is... a lady, Miss Edith Gates'. She was recognised at Association and at National level. She was already well established as minister of a Baptist Church and further events would demonstrate she was fully gifted for the task. This could not now be gainsaid.

Chapter 5: Formal Agreement

Although the national MRC of November 1922 noted that Gates was settled as pastor of a Baptist church and was entered on the Probationers' List, no discussion of the decision took place. However, the precedent was set; women had been entered for the first time on the list of Baptist Union ministers, albeit as probationers. They were by implication moving towards full ministerial accreditation. A woman Baptist minister? The matter was far from resolved in the minds of many.

The whole denomination was now startled into discussion by the action of Gates, Living-Taylor and Hedger and those in the Union, Associations and Colleges who affirmed them. The national MRC was suddenly aware that more applications from women would come. At a special meeting in October 1924, they finally addressed the issue directly and called the attention of the BU Council 'to the numerous questions involved'. They proposed setting up a Committee of Enquiry 'into the principle of admitting women to the accredited list and the various contingencies arising'.[1]

Discussion began about the principle; not least among the women of the denomination. As Mrs Rose had done, they raised their concern about the particular case of Violet Hedger. Although prepared and fully qualified, Hedger 'was unable to find a sphere of service'.[2] One question asked was; do the churches want women ministers at all? Further questions were, as ever, about finance. Will women ministers

---

[1] *BU Minutes,* MRC Special Committee, 17 October 1924, p. 441.

[2] *BU Minutes,* Baptist Women's League (Committee), 18 November 1924, p. 603.

be supported by the recently organised Sustentation Fund? Will they have the usual pension rights? Edith Gates was already receiving a grant of £33 a year from the Fund through the Oxfordshire Association.[3] Lizzie Hughes, Frank Walkey and her other Oxfordshire supporters had decided that Edith should be helped. The finance issues precipitated the appointment by the BU of a small representative group 'to examine the whole subject and report to the Council'.[4]

A lengthy and complex debate took place in the Baptist Union 'involving many and large questions'. Edith Gates was named in the very centre of the discussion, along with the two other women ministers already listed as probationers. She was a symbol of slow but significant change. The BU Council accepted the Committee of Enquiry's *Report Into The Admission of Women to the Baptist Ministry* in February 1926.[5] The report stated that 'it would be contrary to Baptist belief and practice to make sex a bar to any kind of Chistian service' and that this principle 'would in the opinion of the Committee, be generally approved'. (See Appendix 4)

However, that was not exactly the point. Women's ministry seen as 'Christian service' in general, was strongly affirmed, but the issue was practical, not theological. It was about the admission of women to the Accredted List with consequent privileges, notably financial support where needed and pension arrangements: Sustentation and Superannuation. The solicitor to the Baptist Union was consulted and returned the opinion that,

---

[3] *BU Minutes,* MRC Special Committee, 14 September 1925, p. 323.

[4] *BU Minutes,* Council, 18 November 1924, extract of MRC Minutes 28 May 1925 p. 98.

[5] *BU Minutes,* Council, 9-10 February 1926, pp. 789-793 and see Appendix 4.

if a woman's name is placed on one or other of the Ministerial Lists any payment from the Sustentation Fund is perfectly valid.[6]

The fact that Gates (with her two fellow travellers) was already named in the *Baptist Union Handbook* meant she was to be regarded as an accredited minister and should receive the associated benefits; Sustentation and Superannuation.

The decision was made by the national Council in February 1926. A separate Accredited List for women was to be published to be titled 'List of Women Pastors'. Some matters needed to be resolved about the precise way in which money from the two funds was made available, but it was a significant moment. The Baptist Union was saying 'yes' to the accredited ministry of women.[7]

---

[6] Letter from Cecil B Rooke, 6th October 1925, in *BU Minutes*, 9-10 February 1926.

[7] *BU Minutes,* Council, 9-10 February 1926, pp. 789-793.

Chapter 6: Opposition and Resignation

A woman accredited as a probationer by the Union and in post as a local 'pastor' was merely the start of the journey. Gates had personally to win the ultimate recognition of the national MRC. She also had to convince certain individuals in the Oxfordshire Association. As ever, and very soon, opposition to her ministry took shape as a battle over money. The

Little Tew members were not giving sufficient for their pastor's support, which was a household of two. The Trustees of the church asked the Association to assist, but no money was available. The matter sparked disagreement. The Alden Fund, an endowment to help in paying ministers' stipends, had recently included money for the support of Philip Ward at Little Tew. The co-trustees, Mr Burden and Mr C V Wilkins, questioned continuing the payment of the grant to Edith Gates. The Association Committee wrote to the

17. Mr C. V. Wilkins

church; if the Little Tew members would do more they in turn would seek further help. It was also reported that Burden 'did not agree with paying the whole endowment to Miss Gates'. The Committee asked Wilkins, the co-trustee, to go and tell him to 'hand over the whole amount to Miss Gates'. Mrs Hughes and Frank Walkey were present at this decision.[1]

---

[1] *OBA Committee Minutes*, 19th October 1921.

In her own church Gates 'was subject to constant irritation from two quarters'. Certain individuals were seeking to remove her. Her patience was tried and her continuing ministry in jeopardy. In 1922 she resigned the pastorate of Little Tew and Cleveley, to take effect on 31st March. 'The circumstances were discussed' in the Association Committee and it was decided to consult the BU solicitor on the legal position. They also wrote to Gates 'that the association is behind her and hopes she will stay'.[2] Matters were gradually, although painfully resolved. The deacons who opposed her resigned. She reconsidered her decision.

At a subsequent Committee meeting,

> Mr C.V. Wilkins reported that he presided at a church meeting which unanimously requested Miss Gates to continue her ministry, and she had agreed to do so for the present. The church had agreed to take up weekly offerings and had appointed 3 younger deacons to assist the one surviving deacon. And the treasurer of the endowment had come into line and was willing to treat Miss Gates as he had treated Mr Ward. The Church had further agreed to raise £40 for Miss Gates instead of £20, in addition to the endowment.[3]

Edith Gates was winning support and with it the battle for women's ministry: she was to be treated the same as the previous male minister; a unanimous call signalled great acceptance; the raised stipend money reflected growing congregations; appointment of three younger deacons pointed to a confident new start.

However, this period was not free of personal stress and cost. Without the firm backing of the Oxfordshire Association all would have been lost. In addition, by 1922 Mrs Mary Gates, still in Belmont, was 70 and at one point it became 'extremely doubtful whether Miss Gates would

---

[2] *OBA Committee Minutes*, 24th January 1922.
[3] *Minutes OBA,* 26 April 1922.

be able to stay another winter owing to the state of her mother's health'.
[4] Edith's brother George had emigrated to Canada so was not available
to help. It would fall to the two sisters to provide care. Removal back
to Belmont would have brought a sad and early end to their fruitful
ministry at Little Tew. Finally it was agreed that Mrs Gates should
come to Little Tew and she spent the last five years of her life in the
commodious manse with her daughters. She died in 1929 and was
honoured in the church Annual Report.

> On Sunday morning November 25th our pastor's mother
> Mrs Gates was called to be with the Saviour she loved so
> well. Ever since she came to reside amongst us she has been
> a source of inspiration to our church, both by her prayers
> and presence in the church.[5]

Edith rode these storms and continued to exercise her ministry
effectively, in Little Tew and Cleveley and beyond.

Determined and astute

From her earliest days Gate's ministry had a strong emphasis on
children and young people. Elizabeth led the flourishing Sunday
School. By 1925 with numbers of children increasing they were ready
to expand. They needed a schoolroom. She looked at her chapel with
its sanctuary, which seated 150 and saw the derelict thatched cottages
next door. Here was possible space for the expanding numbers.

As soon as the cottages became available, she was able to secure them
'through the good offices of a third person'. To raise the £30 needed to
complete the purchase, C. V. Wilkins, one of her supporters in the
Oxfordshire Baptist Association, promised to help.

---

[4] *Minutes OBA,* 26 April 1922.
[5] *OBA Annual Report 1929,* p. 11.

Miss Gates asked if the committee could see its way to make a grant. The committee felt it would be better to collect the required sum privately among friends of the association. It congratulated Miss Gates on securing the cottage, and appointed Mr R. R. Alden to cooperate with Mr Wilkins in raising the £30.[6]

18. Little Tew Village with chapel and converted schoolroom, 1960.

The school hall was created from this property in 1925 by Earnest Warr, a local builder.[7] Later help was also forthcoming through a loan to provide suitable flooring. The Association Annual Assembly in 1931 'resolved to make a loan free of interest to Little Tew for the flooring

---

[6] *Minutes OBA,* 1st May 1922.
[7] Price, Francis. www.littletew.org.uk/download2/A History of Little Tew.pdf [Accessed 9.2022].

of the school room on the usual terms of repayment'.[8] Sadly, the floor gave way dangerously only few years later.[9] The boards may have been new, but undermining rot or unscrupulous worms did severe damage.

19. The converted cottages/School Room today.

In spite of this setback, the number of children at the two churches rose steadily until in 1929 there were 80 children and 7 teachers. The extra space was very well used by the church.

Progress in the schoolroom project illustrates Gates' much needed determination as well as her astute business sense. She dealt firmly and politely with the Rural District Council over her plans for the empty cottage. She wrote to inform them of the modest development. There was division of opinion among the councillors. Some believed wrongly

---

[8] *OBA Minutes,* May 19 and 20, 1931 p. 142.
[9] *OBA Annual Report, 1938,* p. 19.

that their permission was needed and wanted to block the plan. After debate at the Council meeting a decision was deferred.[10]

Gates saw the press report of this discussion and acted within a week. She had enquired of the Baptist Union solicitor and discovered that the need for planning permission had lapsed. The change of use was legal. She wrote to the newspaper to contradict the misinformation; she did not need anyone's permission. She also made it clear directly to the Clerk that Council 'reaction was not necessary'. This was a woman not to be dealt with unfairly, especially where her church and its children was concerned. In any case, she concluded, 'the cottage is now in progress of being demolished. Yours very truly'.[11]

---

[10] *Oxfordshire Weekly News,* Wednesday 18 February 1925, p. 2.
[11] Correspondence, Little Tew and Cleveley Baptist Church. To the Editor of *The Oxfordshire Weekly News*, 25th Feb. 1925, p. 2.

Chapter 7: Wider Ministry

Gradually Edith Gates began to make her mark as a gifted pastor and as an accredited Baptist minister in waiting. She was active in Baptist life beyond her two village churches and beyond the Baptist community. She travelled to the 28th Annual Meeting of the North Cotswold Free Church Council where she was present with other ministers at the preceding 'fraternal'. She now was taking her place, named alongside her male colleagues, in her status as a probationer Baptist minister.[1] Soon we see her being publicly titled 'the Rev Edith Gates'.[2]

Despite the early hesitancy of many she found growing acceptance and wider influence. In 1923 she was elected President of the Cotswold Sunday School Union,[3] she engaged regularly with the Oxfordshire Baptist Association and was elected to the General Committee in 1924. No doubt with her own experience in mind, she sat on the Association 'Commission of inquiry into [the] working of [the] Ministerial Settlement and Sustentation scheme'. She acted as secretary to the Women's Missionary Auxiliary of the Baptist Missionary Society. But she was taking on too much and this last role was a step too far and she soon decided she was 'unable to continue'.[4] Her wider work required travel and therefore finance, so she applied for a travel grant from the Association. They gave five pounds from the Sustentation Fund for

---

[1] *Oxfordshire Weekly News,* Wednesday, 1st Nov. 1922, p. 5.
[2] *Cheltenham Chronicle,* Saturday 3rd May 1924, p. 2.
[3] *Oxfordshire Weekly News*, Wednesday, 27th June 1923, p. 4.
[4] *Minutes OBA,* May 27th, 1924, pp. 10 and 19; December 11th, 1924, p. 24; March 2nd, 1925, p. 29.

ministers' stipends.[5] The Association Committee offered her and the church strong encouragement, as is demonstrated by other regular grants from this fund: £38 in 1926, £55 in 1927 with further renewed and increased grants up to 1929 and beyond.[6]

All this was taking place in the probationary period of Gates' ministry. She still needed to demonstrate formally to the officials of the denomination that she had the skills and ability to be an accredited minister. Melbourn Aubrey, the secretary of the Baptist Union, as he was required for all probationers, sent a letter asking the Association Committee for their report on 'the pastoral efficiency of the Rev Edith Gates'. The Committee's response speaks much of her gifts and character; 'the secretary was instructed to reply to it in eulogistic terms'.[7]

It is not surprising that they responded in this way. An eyewitness account about Gates' impressive ministry is found in a 1977 survey of non-conformist chapels carried out for the Oxfordshire County Council. The author recalled that,

> At Little Tew a 95-year-old lady, as bright as a button, described how three or four hundred people would fill the chapel on Sundays, singing hymns and saying prayers and listening outside to the Reverend Edith Gates, a woman preacher. This all happened over 30 years ago.[8]

---

[5] *Minutes OBA,* October 7th, 1924, p. 23.

[6] *Minutes OBA*, June 22nd, 1926, p. 49, May 17th, 1927, p. 63; May 28th, 1928, pp. 98 and 117.

[7] *Minutes OBA,* May 28th, 1928, p. 98.

[8] Report of Mr and Mrs Eustace, Minutes of the Parish Survey Meeting 27th November 1977 in *Oxfordshire Archaeological Unit Letter, No 1*, Jan 1978 https://library.thehumanjourney.net/296/1/NewsletterOAUJan1978No.1.pdfA.pdf [Accessed 9.2022].

The Little Tew Chapel seated only 150 and might often have been 'overflowing'. However, we may assume that with the passing years of memory, this elderly lady recalled mainly one specific occasion, as when the church hosted the Oxfordshire Baptist Association Annual Meetings in September 1927, when the church and the recently completed schoolroom would indeed have been packed with a large congregation. However, this account mirrors other evidence that points to a lively weekly ministry and a flourishing church, with singing and praying and effective preaching, in the first period of Gates' pastorate.

She was inevitably favoured by organisers as a preacher at events for women. In October 1928 she travelled to Chesham for 'Women's Sunday' at Hinton Baptist Church, where she was the preacher for an afternoon meeting and for 'a splendid congregation' at the normal evening church service. The women of a local church might initiate an invitation, but the church then invited her, as here, to preach for another service. On this occasion it was reported,

> She has the distinction of being the first Baptist lady
> preacher and has held the post of minister to the churches
> of Little Tew and Cleveley for the past ten years.

Even in this enthusiastic report of two 'impressive' meetings the language was guarded; she was 'the first Baptist lady preacher' holding 'the post of minister'.[9] After making her mark for ten years there was still caution; a continuing deep reluctance to acknowledge her equal standing and title as a woman Baptist minister.

Considerable evidence exists that Gates travelled far in response to invitations to preach. She was not only interesting to many as the first woman Baptist minister of a church, but she soon gained a reputation as a stimulating and engaging communicator. In 1929 she was elected vice-President, and therefore President-in-waiting of the expanded and

---

[9] *Buckinghamshire Examiner*, 26 Oct 1928, p.2

renamed Oxfordshire and East Gloucestershire Baptist Association.[10] Consequently, her sphere of ministry widened even further. In May 1930 she was at Devonshire Avenue, Portsmouth.[11] In November at Wendover for a Women's Sunday, where 'her message was listened to with very great interest', and she conducted 'a very impressive Communion Service'.[12] She was invited for a 'Women's Own' Sunday in Nottingham, preaching morning and evening in April, 1932. Based on the 'novel experience of having an ordained woman preacher in the pulpit' the church invited her again for the following year.[13] Invitations of this kind came during the years of her subsequent ministry from many churches. In 1939, on the eve of war, she was at Uxbridge, preaching on 'The World's Need'.[14]

Wherever she went Gates was remarked upon as one of the very few ordained women ministers among the Baptists.

She favoured the West Country in holiday times and went with her sister and friends to stay at 'Shackhays', a guest house in Combe Martin, Devonshire. Naturally, the party attended the Baptist Church on Sundays. Local press reported and drew attention to her ministry at Little Tew and Cleveley. On one occasion the report noted 'that for sixteen years she has carried on all the duties of the sacred calling in the two Churches named, which are situated [in] Oxfordshire'. As a regular visitor to Combe Martin, she was drawn in and asked to address the 'United Bible Class'. Even on holiday she was willing to be of service in some way to the host church.[15]

---

[10] Renamed in 1929.

[11] *Portsmouth Evening News*, 17 May 1930, p. 7.

[12] *Bucks Herald*, Friday 14 November 1930, p. 5.

[13] *Nottingham Journal*, 2 April 1932, p.4, *Nottingham Evening Post*, 4 April 1932, p.5 and *Nottingham Journal*, 1 April 1933, p. 4.

[14] *Uxbridge & W. Drayton Gazette*, 24 Feb. 1939, p. 17.

[15] *North Devon Journal*, 13 July 1933 p. 7 and 28 June 1934, p. 8 and 16 July 1936, p. 8.

Union and Association

Gates demonstrated deep and continuing commitment to the Baptist
Union and local Association life and recognised the value and support
of such connections. Little Tew hosted the Association Autumnal
Meeting in 1927. At the business meeting she raised the matter of her
church trust and sought advice. She pointed out that all the trustees were
dead. It was therefore agreed, at her instigation, to bring the Little Tew
properties under the trusteeship of the Baptist Union Corporation.[16]

She was ready to let her name be proposed for election as President of
the Oxfordshire and East Gloucestershire Baptist Association. She was
elected in 1929 to serve in 1930-31. In this role she was the first woman
minister, preceded by one other woman, her supporter Mrs Lizzie
Hughes. The ambiguous minute of this election may point to continuing
hesitancy among the voters (or of the minute taker) at the annual
assembly. It reads, 'ultimately the Rev Edith Gates being elected', as if
there had been uncertainty, or a contest.[17] In her role as President she
was, for that year and sometimes subsequently, the chair of the
Association Committee. She sat for many years as a member of the
Committee. Her sister Elizabeth sometimes also was present.

Gates was one of the founders of the Oxfordshire and East
Gloucestershire Baptist Women's Prayer Circle.[18] The 'Prayer Circle'
movement began among women in 1932. It was taken up by churches
or groups of churches such as the Baptists in the Oxford area. Gates was
local President in 1945-46 and represented the 18 affiliated groups at
ecumenical events. It was through connection with other Women's
Prayer Circles that she was on a rare occasion during her retirement
engaged as preacher at a Women's Sunday in Wells. Gates was the
special speaker, and 'her messages throughout the day bore evidence of

---

[16] *Minutes OBA,* September 22nd, 1927, p. 76.

[17] *Minutes of Oxfordshire and East Gloucestershire Baptist Association,* May 28th
1929, p. 124.

[18] *Banbury Guardian,* 10th Oct. 1946, p. 5.

her wide experiences in Christian work, both at home and abroad'. [19]
The reference to 'abroad' is certainly hyperbole. There is no evidence
that Gates ever travelled beyond the UK in her ministry or for leisure.[20]

A further insight into her broad sympathy and readiness to serve comes
from the later war years. The Enstone Bomber Command Airfield, built
in 1942, was only three miles away from Little Tew. Edith formed a
connection with the WAAF stationed there and thus found yet another
sphere of work.[21]

---

[19] *Wells Journal,* 23 Feb., 1951, p. 4-5.

[20] In C.S. Lewis, *Collected Letters Volume II* (HarperCollins, 2004, p. 616) a letter
of May 1944 'to Edith Gates' is published. Exploration of the originals held in the
Marion E. Wade Centre at Wheaton College, Illinois, shows this is another person,
Edith Pearl Gates, living in Youngstown, Ohio.

[21] *OBA Annual Report 1944,* p. 21.

Chapter 8: Elizabeth Gates

There is little public or formal record of Edith's older sister Elizabeth (1880-1960) usually named 'Miss B. Gates', but she was a highly significant part of Edith Gates' story. The life-long companion of Edith, their lives overlapped almost exactly for 80 years. They always shared a home: in Belmont during childhood, then in Little Tew and finally in Weston-Super-Mare. In her younger years she had 'private means', from her father and then her brother's business.[1] She and Edith lived in the Little Tew manse from 1911, at first for seven years as guests of the Wards, then a further 32 years during Edith's ministry. In the *National Register* Edith's personal occupation was marked as 'Baptist Minister', while for Elisabeth it was 'unpaid domestic duties'.[2] They were a team of two, living off private income and one minister's stipend.

However, Elizabeth's duties were much wider than her 'domestic' role. She was deeply committed to supporting her sister, but she had a unique ministry of her own. This was a close and equal partnership from which they were never apart. Local recollection in Oxfordshire told that there were 'two Miss Gates' living in the Baptist manse; the Rev Edith Gates, the minister, with 'her sister acting as organist'.[3] The music was merely one aspect of her service. She was also 'church secretary' for the two churches during the whole of Edith's time as minister. She was commended as an adept administrator and she had an office in the chapel building.[4] She represented the Little Tew and Cleveley churches

---

[1] *1911 Census of England*, Surrey, Belmont, Mary Gates household.
[2] *The National Register*, 1939, EZEP, Chipping Norton, Little Tew.
[3] Price, Francis, www.littletew.org.uk [accessed 20.8.20].
[4] *OBA Annual Report,* 1947, p. 23.

as early as 1916, as a 'Messenger' and on other local occasions.[5] Most references to her are in connection with the Sunday Schools at the two chapels. These flourished from the time of the arrival of Philip Ward and the sisters in 1911 and continued in subsequent years under the specific leadership of Elizabeth Gates.[6]

Eventually Elizabeth was elected to the Oxfordshire Baptist Association committee in her own right (1940) and was then regularly present.[7] She partnered Edith in the formation of the Women's Prayer Circle and continued as a member of it for the 17 years of its existence. She was honoured by name at the celebration marking 28 years of Edith's ministry where special mention was made of 'the help rendered to her by her sister'. Among the tributes, the influential Mrs J. (Lizzie) Hughes of New Road, Oxford, then aged 84, declared 'that the influence of the Misses Gates had spread far and wide throughout the country'.[8]

Theirs was an immensely effective ministry partnership of two differing personalities. Edith was clearly the leader and preacher. She was tall and imposing. Elizabeth was shorter, a warm and more motherly figure.[9] She was self-effacing, standing in the background of the existing records, but mentioned as being often present. Her words were never recorded, but the influence she exerted in her own way was unmistakeable. Together they were eminently successful.

---

[5] Funeral of Baptist layman, Alderman Theo Clark, *Banbury Advertiser,* Wednesday, 18 April 1945, p.1; *OBA, Annual Report,* 1916.

[6] *OBA Annual Reports,* 1918, p. 21, 1925, p. 9, 1927, p. 7.

[7] *OBA Minutes,* May 22nd 1940, p. 14.

[8] *Banbury Guardian,* 16 May, 1946, p. 3.

[9] Interview with Ray Green, Weston-Super-Mare, July 2020.

20. Elizabeth Gates seated with Edith and Frank Walkey at the opening of the School Room 1925

Chapter 9: The Beginning of the End

Elizabeth was in the habit of using a bicycle to get to her duties. From the manse it was a mile to the Little Tew chapel and five miles to the Cleveley chapel. Even today these are narrow by-roads, they were more dangerous at that time. It was exactly the time when the highest ever number of serious accidents on UK roads was recorded.[1] One afternoon in 1943 Elizabeth, by now 63, 'met with an unfortunate accident while cycling home from the Cleveley women's meeting'. A few years later we read that she 'met with a serious accident and is in hospital'. The second accident was clearly much more damaging, and it is safe to assume it was another cycling accident. She recovered after some months and was able to return to her duties the following year.[2] However, there were troubling consequences. Elizabeth's absences from her church work and her understandable loss of confidence and efficiency spelled the end of this period of the sisters' lives. In addition, Edith herself now 61, also had an unspecified 'accident' in 1943. For Edith, long periods of anxiety over her sister's health, the extra burden upon her of care at home and the increasing age of them both meant that her time in ministry at Little Tew was coming to an end.

The beginning of Edith Gates' ministry at Little Tew was unique and exciting, challenging and pioneering. Its prime was widely honoured and divinely blessed. At its end, we find a significant change of mood. There are clear signs that the spirit had gone out of her. Both sisters were effectively out of action in the Association, frequently missing

---

[1] In 1941 there were 9,169 fatalities.

[2] *OBA Annual Reports,* 1943, p. 21, 1947, p. 23, 1947, p. 22, 1948, p. 22. *Women's Prayer Circle Minutes,* April 7th, 1943 and July 3rd, 1947

from meetings and therefore missing the personal affection and support
of previous years. Edith had also resigned from the Women's Prayer
Circle, reasoning there were 'others who could do the work better than
she could'. This is not the Edith Gates of her early ministry. The
financial accounts of the church were being neglected and there were
'several remarks by the auditor, who had not signed the schedule.'[3] No
annual reports on the church appeared for 1949 or 1950; the church (and
the sisters) drew a veil over the difficulties. The new Central Area
Superintendent, William Miller, reported delicately on Little Tew and
Cleveley that 'the position here was a little unfortunate' and suggested
some modest financial help.[4]

By the end of 1949 Miller told the Association Committee,

> Edith Gates was concluding her long ministry at Little Tew
> and Cleveley. He had sought to arrange some means by
> which the Association could acknowledge the service
> rendered by Miss Gates, but owing to personal difficulties,
> this had proved impossible.[5]

Something was happening to Edith Gates beyond the particular and
practical difficulties of health, church and home, something which
affected her deeply in the last years of her ministry. She was more
lonely than before. Lizzie Hughes her strong and loyal mentor had died
in 1946. In 1942 her long-time, deeply committed supporter, Frank
Walkey retired from being the General Superintendent of the Central
Area. He still lived not far away, and continued with informal personal
support, but without his leading presence Gates' relationship with her
former friends and supporters in the Oxfordshire area began to fade.
Then in December 1949 Walkey died. It may be concluded that the
harsh criticism of some and the continuing inability of many churches
and leaders to accept the public ministry of a woman told in her

---

[3] *WPC Minutes,* July 3rd, 1947 and *OBA Executive Minutes,* April 12th, 1949.
[4] *OBA Minutes,* Sept. 20th, 1949, p. 219.
[5] *OBA Minutes,* January 21st, 1950, p. 221.

emotions. She was without her main supporters and their obvious successors were not equipped to help her.

A further incident points to the conclusion that Gates had begun to retire, in fact to retreat into her own world. The Women's Prayer Circle Committee accepted her resignation as their secretary in July 1947. It was more than a year before they took note of it and agreed that 'a bag' should be given to Edith at the forthcoming women's rally.[6] Gates wrote a letter indicating that 'she would prefer not to have a presentation'. In response a reply, signed by the members of the Committee was sent 'stating appreciation of her work in the past and asking her support in the future.' Such support was not forthcoming and within a year the Women's Prayer Circle was dissolved.[7] If appreciation and gratitude was less than heartfelt, after so many years of devoted service, Edith did not want mere formality.

The situation in the churches at Little Tew and Cleveley 'was such as to give cause for anxiety' and 'there were problems to be faced'.[8] The two sisters had ceased functioning. They were aged 67 and 69 respectively, beyond the normal retirement age of 65 for both men and women at the time. They had been house-hunting in the West Country and were packing to go to Weston-Super-Mare. They moved early in 1950 to 'Brean View', a bungalow in the Hillcote Estate on the outskirts of the town. They enjoyed ten years of retirement together, as well as the company and help of their friend and house companion, George Dean.

---

[6] *WPC Minutes,* Sept. 14th, 1949.
[7] *WPC Minutes,* July 1947, Sept. 14th, 1948 and Jan. 27th, 1950.
[8] *OBA Minutes,* January 21st and February 4th, 1950, p. 221.

Chapter 10: Edith Gates' Preaching

There is little documented material to show the stye and content of Gates' preaching. What records exist of her sermons show a fair consistency in method and style as well as the common response of great appreciation. Part of this respect was because of her unique position as a woman preacher and pastor. She was discernibly conscious of that factor. Even so, based on a few short accounts, the success of her preaching locally and its wide appreciation is fully justified.

In 1923 Gates was elected President of the Cotswold Sunday School Union. The meetings that year were in Little Tew and the occasion was the 117th anniversary of their Sunday School. In a summary of the presidential address, we have a first record of her views and her communication style. As usual, the newspaper report first noted that she was 'the first lady to hold the office'. Speaking on the importance of co-operation in Sunday School work Gates said,

> that the child was of supreme importance and that Christ exemplified this when He called the little child and set it in their midst. In their Sunday School work there must be co-operation between the teacher and the scholar. The teachers must let the child see that they are human, and they would gain its confidence and respect. They must have the co-operation of the Church. There must be an indissoluble link

between pastor, deacons and the Sunday School officials.
Lastly, there must be the co-operation of the parents.[1]

The notes she sounded in this address are present in later reports of her
preaching. The thought was Christ-centred; directly rooted in the gospel
accounts of the life of Jesus. On this occasion she picked out key words
of Jesus which show his attitude to children and she pointed to his
example which we are to follow. The thought was practical in focus;
she noted several measures for co-operation and mutual responsibility.
The mood was natural and human; her words create a sense of her own
humanity, which she urged the teachers also to display. It was corporate
in application; she stressed how every level of the congregation has a
part to play in the united task. Finally, her thought reached beyond an
immediate church context; parents are encouraged to co-operate.

Even in this short, second-hand report of her preaching, we can hear the
notes being struck, and the thoughtful style used, which made her
ministry appreciated and greatly beneficial in the churches of Little Tew
and Cleveley and beyond.

A further example is from October 1927. At the Chesham Baptist
Church Women's Sunday she was the preacher for an afternoon and an
evening service. Her first address of the day was on 'the power of
influence'. As might be expected in the context of that particular
occasion, as well as the still prevalent theology of 'separate spheres' for
men and women, she stressed 'woman's influence in the home'. The
report noted how 'her words were marked by sincerity and earnestness'.
It was recorded that at the evening service she preached to 'a splendid
congregation on the words of the Benediction'. At this service, as is
evident from other reported sermons, she spoke 'with a conviction
which held the people to the last'. A similar Women's Own event at
Great Missenden saw her give a 'very helpful address' at the evening

---

[1] *Oxfordshire Weekly News*, Wednesday, 27 June 1923, p. 4.

public meeting on 'going the second mile'. In this address she sustained a practical focus in her sermon, once again based on the words of Jesus.[2]

The only other record of Edith Gates' preaching is from May 1931. We can explore more detail of this sermon from three existing separate sources. She had been elected President of the Oxfordshire and East Gloucestershire Baptist Association. At the Assembly meetings in May 1931 the retiring president, L. H. Alden, welcomed her with pleasure during the preliminary items, commenting that 'what he knew of Miss Gates filled him with admiration'. He spoke of her 'pluck' and of her work in Little Tew as 'wonderful'.

The account of Gates' response tells that,

> Although she was not the first lady president, she believed she was the first lady minister president. She came from the smallest church in the Association, but they were doing God's work and all were equal in His sight. She was there that day because of three things, firstly, by the grace of God, secondly by the influence of a godly father and mother, and thirdly by the cooperation of her sister.[3]

Mrs Lizzie Hughes, Gates' respected supporter, joined in the welcome especially from the women. She complimented the two sisters on their devotional work and 'how they gave inspiration and guidance to the young men of the village'. There were several references at this time to a group of spiritually eager young men in the Little Tew church. One report stated, 'A special feature is the getting together [of] all the lads in the village.' They met weekly at the manse and were responsible for music in the evening services.[4] In response to Hughes' remark about them, Gates said she did indeed have young men in her church, but 'she had some young women too, and some old men and women.' It is worth

---

[2] *Bucks Herald,* 22 Mar 1929, p.13.

[3] *Banbury Advertiser,* 21 May 1931, p. 5.

[4] *OBA Annual Reports,* 1913, p. 22.

noting here that, even from a friend and supporter, she was not going to let pass without comment the mildest implication that her 'young men' were of more worth than her 'young women', or older people, either men or women. She is deeply self-aware and incisive in the cause of gender equality and inclusion.

The Presidential Address

Three reports exist of Gates' Presidential Sermon for her year of Association office. The *Banbury Advertiser* recorded details of the Annual Meeting and published notes of her 'outspoken address' on 'The Attitude of Christ to the Nation', which 'was listened to by a full church and was most suggestive and helpful'. [5] A second report is fuller, from a different hand, and is arguably more discerning.[6] The third source is the address written up and shortened by Gates herself for the Annual Report of the Association for that year.[7] These are reproduced in full in the appendices.

For this account the three records have been compared and combined and an attempt made to reconstruct the words of the text as it was preached by Edith Gates.

A Reconstructed text

'I have never prepared a sermon unless I have asked the Holy Spirit to guide me. Last night was no exception and I believe that this subject has been given by God:

'The Attitude of Christ to the Nation.'

'The title might sound rather wide, but when it is boiled down it takes in everyone. The nation is a big thing, but we

---

[5] *Banbury Advertiser,* 31st May 1931, p. 5
[6] Report on Annual Assembly, *OEGBA Minutes,* May 19 and 20, 1931, p. 144.ff.
[7] *OBA Annual Reports,* 1931, p. 1f.

need to remember that nations are comprised of individuals. There is a cause today which is very much on the minds of thinking people, and that is the *League of Nations*. The conference at Geneva is a big thing,[8] yet every individual can have a share in its work, a share in deciding what the *League of Nations* should do. The *League* is a great thing, but it is no new thing. Seven hundred and sixty years before Christ one nation had the same idea as the world today; that there should be no more war. But how is it to be accomplished? Only in so far that the Spirit of Christ is shown in our actions. The attitude of Christ to the nation was prophesied in Isaiah. We read 'He shall startle many nations'. And has he not done this? In his earthly life he was constantly startling those about him. There was something pretentious,[9] something volcanic about him. He startled people at the time of his birth and up to the time of his death and glorious resurrection. I want to illustrate this by three points – Jesus' methods, his speech, and his deeds.

'Firstly, there is his methods. The Jewish conception of Messiah was that he would make deliverance by conquest, but Christ's conception was by sacrificial and dying love on the cross. He was expected by the Jews to come as a conquering prince, but he came as the meek and lowly Jesus, the son of a carpenter, not born in a royal palace, but in a manger in a stable. All his life He was startling people. He startled men by his life and the nation by his death. He was despised and rejected and died upon the Cross. His death startled them. He startled the nation by his resurrection, and by asking a woman to proclaim the message - 'the Lord is risen'. That was Christ's method. Do

---

[8] Preparatory meetings for the 1932 League of Nations 'Geneva Conference' on disarmament were beginning in 1931.

[9] There is probably an error here. More suitable would be 'presumptuous', or best of all 'sententious'.

you not think the methods of Christ would startle the
Lambeth Conference?[10] They will not allow women
ministers in the Church, but if Christ came to earth might
he not say, 'A woman shall do it'?

'Then think of his speech. Again and again they found the
multitude astonished at his wisdom, for 'he taught as one
having authority'. This was not because of his manner, but
his matter. The comment of the people was, 'Never man
spake like this man.' His speech staggered the Scribes and
Pharisees. He told them plainly, God did not want sacrifices
so much as He wanted obedience. Christ had no
eccentricities. He was no soothing, drawing-room preacher.
If he occupied the pulpits of today he would not be a very
popular preacher. I very much doubt if he would be asked a
second time. What is wanted in the churches today are men
and women not ashamed to preach the counsels of God and
to have the courage of their convictions. The preacher today
who preaches the truth of Jesus will startle society. The
church that practised it would startle the world. People
today might be bored by sermons, or interested, or perhaps
entertained, but scarcely ever startled by them. Take his
attitude towards money; he said it was the most deadly path
for the soul, and he meant exactly what he said. Think of
his teaching on the great doctrine of love, 'Thou shalt love
thy neighbour as thyself', then look at Jesus' parable of the
Good Samaritan. Work it out, think of the moral of the
story. He says, 'Go thou and do likewise.' If this word was
translated into everyday life our nation would be better, it
would turn the world upside down. If it was translated into
everyday life, it would transform business relations.

'I wonder what Christ would say if he saw his servants
acting as masters of ceremonies at a whist drive and dance

---

[10] Lambeth Conference of March 1931. See below.

in a room attached to a church, to raise money for a bazaar. What would he say about the finding of an empty whisky bottle in the schoolroom of a church after the previous night's dance? Then the desecration of the Sabbath; what would Christ say of the Sunday School Superintendent who, as he came out of morning school, asked one of the scholars to go across the road to the shop and buy a Sunday paper for him? If He came personally into our churches to-day I think a good many would be startled. Ministers, deacons, and members need to search their own hearts, as he would search them.

'Lastly, I want you to think how startling Christ was in his deeds. He gave sight to the blind, healing to the sick, and cleansing to the leper and he raised the dead to life. But those were not the most startling things he did. There were his deeds of redeeming love. What more mighty work could be done on earth than the salvation of men and women, the rebirth of a soul, to see men and women 'turn from the power of Satan to God?' And he has left a plan, for you and me to carry out, to try and win lost ones back to him.

'Christ's attitude to the nation is just the same today. What is wanted is more prayer - and faith in the living God. Christ expects us as his followers to show forth his life to others and by doing so to glorify him. I urge you to take heart, so that by his help we win souls for him and bring many into the fold.

'There will be some startling revelations at the Judgment Seat. Christ called the Pharisees 'whited sepulchres' and we all need to search our own hearts. The Church to-day is suffering not so much from antagonism from without as from apathy within. Too many are 'at ease in Zion'. We are about the King's business, and 'the King's business requires haste'. Let us put away doubts and fears and get a fresh grip on this Mighty Christ, who can startle all the world by his deeds of redeeming grace. This is the Christ who we preach. The Christ in whom is infinite resources of power. His promise is, 'Lo, I am with you always'. He will not fail us. Let us then be strong and of good courage. 'I am with thee', says the Lord. Put aside doubts and fears and hang on the promises of Christ. He is the living Lord and His Kingdom will 'stretch from shore to shore, till moons shall wax and wane no more'.

Analysis

The energy and impact of this sermon is apparent, even in a shortened, written, and second-hand form. Gates structured her sermon in a simple classic shape: an introduction, three clear sections, and a concluding appeal and practical challenge. She dealt with the startling nature of Jesus' ministry in its method, its speech, and its redeeming deeds. In the opening she gave an unashamed personal introduction, justifying the theme. Then she found a large canvas of current events on which to place her message, a challenge to personal behaviour and inner motive. She made this move with reference to the struggling *League of Nations*, and by means of the question, 'How is the aim of the *League* going to be accomplished?' She answered it with 'only in so far as the Spirit of Christ is seen in our actions'. Jesus as 'startling' was the uniting theme, expressed in by that striking word, with which she also held together the three sections. She made application from Jesus' startling life, teaching, and saving work.

In applying the first section Gates robustly presented her own 'startling' position as a woman Baptist minister in a man's world. She chided the Anglicans (and through them the Baptists in the congregation in front of her) with her question, 'Do you not think the methods of Christ would startle the Lambeth Conference?' Only a few weeks before, the Committee of the Lambeth Council had presented their report on the October 1930 Conference in which they noted, with satisfaction that the Conference emphatically re-affirmed the decision of the Conference of 1920, that the Anglican Communion cannot admit women to the Priesthood.[11]

Gates' response to this was blunt and ground-breaking. It was also very cleverly crafted. Her line is brilliant in the context; 'If Christ came to earth today, would he not say, "A woman shall do it"?'.

These sentences are classic and very clever rhetoric. First, she did not directly challenge the representative 'Baptists' in front of her. To make her own affirmation she used the Anglicans' recently reaffirmed flat rejection of the priesthood of women. Then she asked a rhetorical question, one she did not intend, or need to deal with at that moment. The hearers were left to answer it in their own minds. Many in the congregation were dubious if not hostile about whether she should be a minister at all. They now had to think of their own answer to her question. Finally, she did not take it upon herself to verbalise the statement to be thought about, she let it fall from the very lips of Jesus. Her method at that moment was indeed 'startling': 'Hear Jesus speak today, 'Would he not say, "A woman shall do it."?'

She did not need to answer her own question. She stood before them that day; a woman, an accredited Baptist minister, an effective pastor for 13 years. She was herself the visible affirmative response to the question. It was at the very least courageous. And it was a model of the startling method of Jesus.

The second section ended with exhortations on drinking, dancing and Sabbath observance, almost inevitable thoughts in the evangelical world of the early 20th century. The best that can be said is that it was Gates' attempt to apply her challenge ethically to the context of her time. The third section explored the power of Christ and his startling

---

[11] The English Church Union and the Lambeth Conference, *The Report of the Committee of the Council, 18th March, 1931*. (London: English Church Union).

redeeming deeds. It led to the conclusion, where she challenged her hearers to greater faith and witness and gave assurance of help if they will 'get a fresh grip on this Mighty Christ'.

The sermon as reported affirms what we noted above in her sermon on children and the church in 1923. Edith Gates' teaching was essentially Christ-centred. It was greatly dependent on the gospel narratives and was immensely practical and relevant. It was also politically aware and in touch with wider church politics. Her own mission on womens' ministry was not delicately set aside so as not to offend, but faced head on, even in a large public context.

She had an eye for a good turn of phrase, a chiming list, or a metaphor. We can note in this 1931 sermon:

> great thing, but no new thing...
> not his manner, but his matter...
> no soothing, drawing-room preacher...
> bored by sermons, interested, entertained, but scarcely startled...
> work it out...
> antagonism from without - apathy from within...
> get a fresh grip on this Mighty Christ...
> hang on the promises of Christ.

These may have been natural expressions to her, but much more likely they are studied and practised, perhaps borrowed. It would not be surprising if, for example, the challenge to 'work it out' was a regular phrase in her preaching after making an appropriate point. In this and many ways she had the ability to involve the hearers and make them respond. We see this skill in her use of metaphors, her rhetorical questions, her practical challenges, and her teasing references. Two or three sermon examples are limited evidence, but we may fairly conclude that this is how she habitually preached. The effectiveness of her ministry in the two small village churches she served is therefore not surprising.

Chapter 11: Retirement and Final Years

In 1950 Edith Gates retired and moved to Weston-Super-Mare with her sister Elizabeth; to the West Country, where they had taken holidays for several years. They lived in Brean View, a three-bedroom detached bungalow with panoramic views of the Bristol Channel, in the airy Hillcote estate off Bleadon Hill. George Dean moved with them from Oxfordshire. He lived with the two sisters until his death in 1959.[1] Dean's family were long time members of the Cleveley chapel. As a young man he partnered Elizabeth in the leadership of the flourishing Cleveley Sunday School and he was listed as an accredited lay preacher of the chapel in 1929 and was elected a deacon.[2] He appeared in the record of a number of events supporting Edith. Dean presided at the 21st Anniversary celebration of her ministry. On this occasion 'presentations were made to the pastor and her sister the secretary... and tokens of love and gratitude for their untiring work by Mr George Dean'. He presided similarly for their 30th Anniversary.[3] Most significant, he is one of the two deacons who signed the strategic letter to the *Baptist Times* pointing out that a woman, Edith Gates, had been their pastor since 1918. He was a deeply loyal supporter of both sisters, and they became very close; to move in with them in their new home at Weston was unusual, but not surprising, particularly if three sources of funding made possible the purchase, or rent, of a very desirable retirement bungalow.

---

[1] Interview with Ray Green, Weston-Super-Mare, July 2020.
[2] *OBA Annual Report*, 1925, p. 9 and 1929, p. 23.
[3] *OBA Annual Report*, 1940, p.23 and 1948, p. 22.

21. Edith's retirement bungalow, Hillcote Estate, Weston-Super-Mare.

Edith, Elizabeth, and George Dean began attending Clarence Park Baptist Church in Weston and were received as members in April 1952.[4] All three were regular in Sunday attendance for the next decade, almost inevitably together, or absent at the same times. Victor Joseph Smith succeeded as pastor in March 1952, and he became a trusted friend, named as one of Edith's executors when she died.

Gates was very quickly approached by the active women's group of the church, the Baptist Women's League. Only four months after moving she was listed as a possible speaker for their devotional meeting, named as 'Miss E. Gates', not 'the Rev Gates' in contrast to the 'Rev' male

---

[4] Green, Ray, *More about Christ's People,* p. 25, and Clarence Park Baptist Church, *Church Meeting Minutes,* April 29th, 1952, p. 377.

ministers in the list. She addressed this meeting in April and December 1951 and in 1952. At the former occasion 'taking as her subject "A Woman" Jesus after the resurrection', the resurrection appearance of Jesus to Mary Magdalene ('go tell the other disciples') and the influence of women in the New Testament. At the latter 'her talk was on the Fatherhood and Motherhood of God in his infinite forgiving love to us his children'. [5] She was quite confident in this setting to address the place of women in the church and the feminine in God.[6] She is listed again as a possible speaker for December that year, but is given a subject. The record shows an early reply to this invitation, marked next to her name is her immediate 'Yes'. She is still eager to preach and to serve if asked. There is no record of her doing so again. Nor, with the exception in 1953 noted below, did she preach on a Sunday in the Clarence Road church, or elsewhere in other local churches.

The incident recorded above, of Edith Gates' unannounced appearance in the pulpit as the preacher one Sunday morning at Clarence Park, Weston-Super-Mare and the consequent written protests must have taken place just before October 1950. In response to the objections of some members, the deacons first decided she should only preach if it was a last resort. The rule was agreed that 'Rev Edith Gates be asked to fill [the] pulpit only if unable to find other supply'. For this we must read 'other male supply'.[7] In fact, in 1953 the deacons reversed the priority, at least for a single occasion. 'Mr Smith had an engagement for Sunday 3rd November and it was decided to invite Rev Edith Gates to conduct the service, failing her Mr Jack White.'[8] The mood regarding women in ministry was changing, albeit almost imperceptibly.

George Dean, supporter and fellow worker of Elizabeth and Edith for almost 50 years, died in September 1959 leaving an estate of £1300 to

---

[5] Clarence Park BC, *Minutes of the BWL Executive Committee*, July 12th, 1950 and *BWL Record of Meetings,* April 4th, 1951

[6] Clarence Park BC, *BWL Record of Meetings,* April 4th, 1951 and Dec. 3rd, 1952

[7] Clarence Park BC, *Deacons Minutes,* 10th October, 1950, p. 166

[8] Clarence Park BC, *Deacons Minutes,* 22nd Sept. 1953

be administered by Edith. Elizabeth Gates died in 1960. She left a legacy of £10,000 to her sister Edith. For the last two years of her life Edith was left to live alone in the bungalow they had enjoyed together. There is less joy in splendid views without the companionship of a sister, or a friend.

Edith Gates died on the 19th of January 1962 at the Royal Hospital Weston-Super-Mare. The Clarence Park minister, Victor Smith, gave written tribute to Edith and to others recently deceased.

> The Rev Edith Gates was the first accredited woman Baptist Minister in our denomination. Her later years of retirement among us brought her the sorrows of bereavement and increasing loneliness. No one in the church, besides the minister, will know the extent of the support given by the 'right hand' without the 'left hand' knowing. So these have gone up from us and we need others to come and take their place that the work they loved may go on. We thank God for them.[9]

Who can measure 'the sorrows of bereavement' that broke upon this courageous, able, and godly servant of Christ?

---

[9] Clarence Park BC, *Monthly Newsletter,* Feb. 1962.

Chapter 12: A Credible Minister of Jesus Christ

This final chapter offers some reflection on the life and ministry of Edith Gates. Others will be better able to evaluate her place in the longer story of church life in Britain, or her significance in the Baptist Union and the arrival of women into its ministry. What interests me for the present is what we might learn from her thirty-two years of unique and effective local church ministry. There is a direct connection between the local success she enjoyed and her influence as a woman Baptist Minister. Without local church success she would be neither credible, nor admired as a pioneer. Her accolades as a woman minister are related to the high regard in which she was held. For her influence to be accepted she needed more than the mundane or common. She had to be good, very good.

So what, I ask, were the elements in her ministry that made it so? What can we understand from her context and relationships, from her skills and character, which might inform a contemporary approach to local church ministry? The lessons are wider than the ministry of women, they apply to anyone. After a hundred years it would be tempting to say that there is not much to learn for our very different 21st century context. However, aspects of her life and ministry are instructive for all time.

Here I have teased out ten lessons for effective ministry based on the life and ministry of Edith Gates. Success never rests on just one thing, certainly not on a mere list of qualities - do this and this and you will prosper. The path to steady value in ministry is more subtle than that, it is more relational and intuitive. But Edith Gates had that touch, whatever it is. From her story I outline some of those elements which made for her manifest success.

1. An admired model

An illuminating moment in my research on Gates was the discovery that Philip Marcus Ward was the direct connection between a young woman from a Surrey village and a small church in rural Oxfordshire. He made it happen. Even more important was the recognition that he was the model of a good Baptist pastor. In all important respects Ward did a good job, first at Belmont, then at Little Tew and subsequently in two further pastorates. He was a model of fine preaching, of zeal for evangelism and winning dedication to the ministry task in its pastoral and management aspects.[1] The relationship between Ward and Gates was clearly a close one. They were fellow workers, but the modelling he offered was deeply reflected in her own life and ministry.

Today mentoring is a significant part of the training of leaders and ministers. The Baptist Union concludes about its mentoring scheme, 'the support of a mentor has proved time and again to be hugely helpful' to Newly Accredited Ministers.[2] Even if mentoring is not formally set up, together with their own essential sense of call, aspiring leaders and ministers usually have in their sight or memory a person who represents for them what they want to become. That person's strengths, their methods, their style, and indeed their weaknesses, are continued in the follower. Where formally set up, often with a contract, mentoring has the added value of regular contact, observation, structured conversation, and feedback. Ward worked it so that Edith would be with him in his new church and would be accessible to such influences. For seven years, from 1911, she lived in the manse and shared fully in his ministry. To observe, participate, discuss, and learn in a close community of that kind shapes a person profoundly. Mentoring aims

---

[1] Obituary, O. D. Wiles, *BU Handbook 1932,* p. 333.

[2] Baptists Together, *Newly Accredited Ministers' Programme*, (20021-22) p. 7.

for the same. Formal or informal it should be a high priority for leaders and ministers.

2. Influential supporters

In the light of her story, we cannot think of Edith Gates without the names of the influencers who surrounded and helped her. These included Lizzie Hughes, lifelong Superintendent of the St Thomas Mission and fellow member of the Oxfordshire Baptist Association Committee, Frank Walkey, Baptist Superintendent of the Central Region, several pastors of New Road Baptist Church such as Ronald Hobling, who supervised her probationary studies, and in later years Victor Joseph Smith, the pastor in Weston-Super-Mare. These, and others less prominent, regularly took up her challenging cause. In various minutes it can be discerned that when crucial early decisions were made about Gates' position, on her future or financial support, Lizzie Hughes and Frank Walkey were present. Where they were not present there is evidence of less conviction about the cause of women.[3] As a Superintendent, Walkey also sat on the national Ministerial Recognition Committee and was able to track Edith's progress. He supported and encouraged her, crucially onto the probationer ministry list in 1922 and finally onto the Accredited List.

The evidence shows that Edith won the high respect of these women and men by her character and her apparent ministry gifts. Her obituary speaks of her as 'this gracious Christian lady',[4] a personal observation that accounts for much in her life. She had to be courageous and very determined as a woman pioneer. She came over to some as 'imposing', even 'severe'.[5] However, there was also softness and grace in her character which won contemporaries to her cause, in her own church and in the area. No Christian leader can make progress without the

---

[3] e.g. OBA Committee Minutes, Oct. 14th 1937 and compare Jan. 17th, 1938.

[4] Unattributed, *BU Handbook,* 1962, p. 362. See Appendix 5.

[5] Interview with Ray Green, Weston-Super-Mare, July 2020 and Green, R., *More about Christ's People at Clarence Park* (Weston-Super-Mare: Ray Green, 2008), p. 25.

sustained support of others. If those supporters are influential there is greater possible blessing. If the support is long sustained, as it was for Edith over many decades, the greater the long-term good. Such support depends on others recognising godly character and gifts and if a minister can obtain it, great strength is to be found.

3. A credible ministry

Credibility is a communal dynamic. You cannot be credible on your own. A leader may be sincere, a person of integrity, with the qualities and character of an inner life displayed in practice. However, for a leader to be credible others must see it and believe it. A minister may carry out all the duties of the pastoral task, but still fail to convince. Then their credibility is undermined and consequently the ability to lead in that specific context. Edith Gates won the confidence of others and gained credibility as a Baptist minister over four decades. In early years she had to fight to be accepted. Some in her own two congregations wanted to remove her and in the Oxfordshire Association a few opposed her. This was not because she was incapable as a minister, it was because she was a woman. Set aside that prejudice and Gates emerges as a highly competent and credible minister of Christ.

To maintain credibility Gates needed adequate gifts for her task. As with any ministry, she succeeded because she had the gifts needed for pastoral leadership in her context. She studied and grew in stature. She had a place in which to develop her skills, first under Philip Ward's mentoring and then on her own, aided by the loyal team that surrounded her. Though not apparently highly educated, Gates was manifestly able, intelligent, and naturally gifted in many ways. Those gifts were more than sufficient for her ministry and leadership at Little Tew and Cleveley and beyond. Any pastor or leader must measure their gifts against the demands of their context. We are to regard ourselves not more highly than we ought to think, but with 'sober judgement'. Credibility and success in ministry follow such judgement.

4. Creative communication

Although we have limited material to assess her teaching, we can see that Edith Gates was an engaging and lively preacher, able in public leadership. It is regularly remarked upon; her words were 'marked by sincerity and earnestness' and had a 'conviction which held the people to the last'.[6] She gave 'a very helpful address',[7] or her sermon 'was listened to with very great interest' and she led a 'very impressive Communion Service'.[8] The impact of her preaching is shown clearly in the accounts of her Presidential Address of May 1931. Her sermons were clearly structured, thoroughly prepared, biblically founded and practically applied. She spoke in natural phrases and expressions. Her line 'the nation is a big thing', which she repeats again about the Geneva conference, is hardly beautiful, but it said what she wanted in ordinary, easy to grasp words. Even filtered through the pens of the reporters, her speech comes over as free flowing and full of life. It is no surprise that at one Church Anniversary they gave thanks for 'the freshness and power of our pastor's preaching for 21 years'.[9]

No Christian minister who hopes to be successful can make an impact without at least some measure of the ability in communication which we see in Edith Gates. Ability to persuade in words, to manage people by persuasion, a capacity to inspire a congregation, the skill to argue strongly for the cause of Christ; all are needed. Edith Gates had the aptitude to carry out these tasks of communication with creativity. The teaching was effective among her adults and among the children and young people of her churches. When she was on duty in Chapel or Sunday School there was life, interest, inspiration, enjoyment. Christlike ministry is in her words. Anyone who aspires to lead and teach today might imitate her with profit.

---

[6] *Buckinghamshire Examiner*, 26 Oct., 1928.

[7] *Bucks Herald,* 22 Mar. 1929, p. 13

[8] *Bucks Herald,* Friday 14 Nov. 1930, p. 5.

[9] *OBA Annual Report,* 1940, p. 23.

5. Social and political awareness

Churches of the early 20th century, particularly evangelical ones, are rightly judged as having become insular, cut off from the social and political context of the time. Gates was widely informed and personally active beyond her church ministry. She used the recent *League of Nations* conferences as a starting point for her 1931 sermon. She was fully aware of current Anglican decisions as she referred to their blank refusal of women's ordination. During the Second World War she took up an opportunity to act as a voluntary chaplain among the WAAFS at nearby Enstone aerodrome.[10] She read local newspapers as well as the *Baptist Times*. She was able to pick up and firmly address the local Council on their misreading of the church's plan for the next-door cottage to be a schoolroom for the Little Tew children.

Social and political awareness hardly needs emphasis as an aspect of Christian mission today, so strong is the call on ministers and church members to be practically involved in community and nation. Edith Gates' story demonstrates deep commitment to her local community, but also to wider questions of justice and social care. She is most obviously a notable model as a determined champion for women's freedom and equality. Such advocacy is still much needed.

6. Intimate family or friends

This element is more difficult to bring forward, since not every minister or leader has the same context of relationships or the depth of support from close family. Having recognised this it is evident that life-long intimacy with her sister Elizabeth was a powerful source of strength to Edith, personally, practically at home, and for her ministry. For many ministers a marriage partner fills that place. Others will cultivate closeness to friends who will meet the same need for friendship, natural companionship, and emotional support. Edith also drew on a much wider circle, including Philip and Lilly Ward and George Dean, the

---

[10] *OBA Annual Report,* 1944, p. 21.

deacon and friend who became house companion to the sisters in Weston Super Mare.

Relationships of this kind are essential for personal growth and emotional health and for balancing life in its complex demands. Family relationships or friendships of such a kind need to be nurtured. They can be cultivated, sustained for life, and so be continually transforming and life-enhancing.

7. Teamwork

No church leader or minister can achieve alone. Gates always worked with a team. In early years at Belmont with Ward she demonstrated her ability as a team player. The teamwork under his leadership continued for seven years in Oxfordshire. Then she used those same skills to lead her own successful team for thirty-two years. Edith was distinctly the leader, able in communication, forthright and actively determined. Elizabeth comes across as a more motherly character, modest and devoted in administrative and pastoral support. The full inclusion of Elizabeth, a very different character, was a great asset as the sisters balanced and complemented each other in the ministry.

After the initial objections and painful resignations of some in the church, groups of loyal friends and deacons formed around her, and worked wisely and faithfully with her for three decades. Among these was George Dean, as noted above. He appears very infrequently in the records, but he was clearly a devoted and invaluable asset to Gates and to the mission of the two chapels for many years. No doubt he was typical of others.

The subject of working teams is a large and complex one, but its essence is to work respectfully and in consultation with others for a common goal in mutually balancing roles. Teamwork and active listening are essential for any kind of ministry or leadership today, particularly in a Baptist congregational context. The subject and practice of teams must be addressed and taken up by a minister who wishes to successfully stay the course for any length of time.

8. Resilience

The record of Edith's story does what most formal accounts of church life do. For understandable and perhaps noble reasons, the minute-takers leave out painful events, overlook failings, omit the names of perpetrators of wrong, and seek lovingly to cover sins. We cannot therefore reconstruct detail of the most agonising parts of her career. Edith clearly suffered much that is not recorded. Yet she pursued her deep sense of call with vibrant determination. She rose above the worst opposition and bore the slights and the cruel language. Her story illustrates some of these moments, albeit in faint shadow. The same was true of Violet Hedger, who rose above rejection and spiteful behaviour.[11] Like her fellow traveller, Edith Gates was resilient. She had the inner strength to recover and rise again, using the variety of human and godly supports that were essential to survive.

No leader or minister of Christ can avoid a measure of such pain and wounds. If as a pastor you want to be like Jesus, at some point you will be crucified.

9. Convincing spirituality

None of this would have been possible without an inner life of genuine faith and prayer. The evidence is slim, her spirituality was ultimately visible only to God and perhaps to those who shared her home. But Gates demonstrated a reliance on and commitment to corporate prayer in the churches she served, which must reflect her personal devotional life. The comments made about her mother are instructive. Edith spoke

---

[11] Violet Hedger was the subject of a paper given by Deborah Rooke on 30 October 2019 at the CBS Day Conference entitled *Baptist Women Through the Centuries Marking the Centenary of Violent Hedger's Admission to Ministerial Training*. This paper is scheduled to be published in 2023.

of the 'influence of a godly father and mother'[12] and the Little Tew church recorded that her mother was an inspiration 'both by her prayers and presence in the church.'[13] Edith's part in the Women's Prayer Circle and its continuation for eighteen years is a significant insight into her spirituality and prayer life. The opening thought of her Presidential Address was that our war-torn world would ultimately be changed only by Christ through the Spirit working in the hearts, minds, and behaviour of each of us. 'What is wanted is more prayer' she said, 'and faith in the living God.' It is commonly understood that failures of leadership and character stem from our weakness at this very intimate point. As for Edith Gates, blessing and sustained good for the church as well as the Christlike discipleship of the minister will be found in that same place.

10. Christ-centred life and teaching

Gates was brought up in an evangelical context in which the gospel meant the salvation of individual sinners through Jesus Christ and his cross. She did not depart from this central theme over her 50 years of service. As we have illustrated, there was much more to her than the basic message, but the essence of this gospel, the centrality of Jesus Christ for life and faith and discipleship was always present. Her intentional work among children and youth in the Oxfordshire villages of her ministry context was to bring them to new birth in him. In her time the church reported and rejoiced over young men, and many others, coming to faith and baptism. From the evidence that exits, Edith's teaching seems often to have been drawn from an incident in the life of Jesus or based on words from his lips. She also was able to pass comment on social and political or ecclesiastical matters. She demonstrably applied the message to the practicalities of life. But her tone, her burden, the centre of her call, was to present Jesus Christ to her hearers and to the whole surrounding community. In this she was manifestly successful.

---

[12] *Banbury Advertiser*, Oxfordshire, 21 May 1931, p. 5.
[13] *OBA Annual Report 1929*, p. 11.

We can profitably ask if the broad themes of the gospel of Christ are still presented clearly by the 21st century church in our worship and teaching. With what do our Sunday hearers, the weekly worshippers, or the passing visitors return home? It can so easily be added burdensome duty, more hard challenge, further religious information. These things are needed in their place. But what most believers need and long for, week by week, is more of Jesus Christ; the grand and unmatched narrative centred on him; a refreshing vision of a merciful and tender God and a saviour who has already done for us all that makes possible the richest and most joyful life of service, both here and hereafter. Pastors and preachers will do well to imitate Edith Gates in this central work in which she excelled.

We still know only a little of the career of Edith Gates, the neglected pioneer of women's ministry. All her life she pursued her vision and call from Christ. It began with teaching difficult boys in a class in the Belmont tin chapel, it developed and grew in serving with Philip Ward, then by wider work in Oxfordshire and beyond. Most notably, she flourished as the woman who was pastor of Little Tew and Cleveley Baptist Church for thirty-two years, leading many to her saviour by her preaching and pastoral care. She invites us still, over a century of years, to 'get a fresh grip on this Mighty Christ, who can startle all the world.'[14]

---

[14] Report on Annual Assembly, *OEGBA Minutes*, May 19 and 20, 1931, p. 144.ff.

Appendices

Appendix 1

The *Banbury Advertiser* reported details of the 129th Annual Meeting of the Oxfordshire and East Gloucestershire Baptist Association which took place at Kings Sutton Baptist Church. It includes record of Gates' welcome as new President and provides notes of her 'outspoken address' on 'The Attitude of Christ to the Nation'.

The President's Address.

'The Rev. Edith Gates said her subject that night had been given her by God. The title of her address might sound rather wide, but when it was boiled down it took in everyone. There was one thing in the minds all to-day - the League Nations - and every individual could have a share in its work. The League of Nations was no new thing. Seven hundred and sixty years before Christ, one nation had the same ideas as the world to-day. How was the aim of the League going to be accomplished? The answer was, by showing the spirit of Jesus Christ. In His earthly life he was always startling people. There was something volcanic about Him, and she wanted to deal with three points connected with His teaching. Firstly, there was His methods. The Messiah was expected by the Jews to come as a prince, but he came as a sufferer in a meek way, born in manger. He was despised and rejected by men and died upon the Cross. All His life He was startling people. His death and resurrection startled them. 'Do you not think the methods of Christ would startle the Lambeth Conference,' said the speaker. They would not allow women ministers in the Church, but if Christ came to earth might He not say, 'a woman shall do it'?

'Christ was always startling in His speech. Again and again they found the multitude were astonished at His wisdom. It was not His manner, but His matter. Christ had no eccentricities, but was no drawing room preacher. There was His story of the Good Samaritan and His attitude towards money. He said it was the most deadly path to the soul, and meant exactly what he said. Nothing would make Christ a soothing teacher, and if He occupied the pulpits today would not be a popular preacher. People to-day might be bored by sermons, or interested, or perhaps entertained, but scarcely ever startled by them. What would he say to a minister acting as M.C. at a dance and whist drive to raise funds to run a bazaar? What would he say about the finding of an empty whisky bottle in the schoolroom of a church after the previous night's dance?

'There would be some startling revelations at the Judgment Seat. Christ called the Pharisees 'whited sepulchres' and they all had need to search their own hearts. The Church to-day was suffering not so much from antagonism from without as from apathy within. Let them all put aside their doubts and fears and hang on the promises of Christ. He was the living Lord and His Kingdom stretch from shore to shore, till moons shall wax and wane no more.'
(*Banbury Advertiser,* 31st May 1931, p. 5.)

Appendix 2

The Minutes of the Oxfordshire and East Gloucestershire Baptist Association Annual Meetings (May 19 and 20, 1931, p. 144.ff) includes a clipping of the text of the presidential sermon of May 19th from another newspaper. It is unreferenced in the minute book, but may be a later edition of the *Banbury Guardian* of 21st May 1931. This longer article, 'The New Lady President from Little Tew', gives an enhanced account of her address, 'The Attitude of Christ to the Nation'.

The Presidential Address

'The Rev Edith Gates observed that she had never prepared a sermon unless she had asked the Holy Spirit to guide her, and she had done so that night with respect to her subject; 'The Attitude of Christ to the Nation.' The title might seem rather wide but when it was boiled down it took in everything. The nation was a big thing, but she wanted them to remember that nations were comprised of individuals. There was a cause today which was very much upon the minds of thinking people, and that was the League of Nations. The conference at Geneva was a big thing, yet every individual could have a share in deciding what the League of Nations should do. After all the League of Nations was no new thing, because 760 years before Christ the nations had the same idea; that there should be no more war. She asked how it was going to be accomplished? Only so far as the spirit of Christ was shown in their actions and she wanted to illustrate this by three points - His methods, speech, and deeds.

'First, let them take his methods. The Messiah was expected to come as a conquering Prince but came as the meek and lowly Jesus, the son of a Carpenter, not born in a royal palace, but in a Manger in a stable. He startled men by his life and the nation by his death. In his resurrection he was also startling. Then think of his speech. Again and again they found the multitude astonished at his teaching, for he taught as one having authority, this was not because of his manner, but his material. The speaker referred to the parable of the Good Samaritan and said if that doctrine of love was acted upon today it would turn the world upside down. If it was translated into everyday life it would transform business relations. What was wanted in the churches today were men and women not ashamed to preach the counsels of God and to have the courage of their convictions. If Christ occupied their pulpit today he would not be a very popular preacher and she very much doubted if he would be asked a second time. The preacher today who preached the truth of Jesus would startle the church and society and the church that practised it would startle the world. She wondered what Christ would say if he saw his servants acting as masters of ceremonies at a whist drive and dance in a school room attached to a church, to raise money for a bazaar. Then with regard to the desecration of the Sabbath she wondered what Christ would say of the Sunday School Superintendent who as he came out of morning school asked one of the scholars to go across the road to the shop and buy a Sunday paper for him? Lastly she wanted them to think how startling Christ was in his deeds. He gave sight to the blind, healing to the sick, and cleansing to the leper. But those were not the most startling things he did. There were his deeds of redeeming love. What more mighty work could be done on earth than the salvation of men and women, the remaking of a soul? Christ's attitude to the nation was just the same today. What was wanted was more prayer and faith in the living God. Christ expected them as his followers to show forth his life to others and by doing so to glorify him. The church today was suffering not so much from the antagonism of those without as from the apathy of those within. Concluding, she urged them to take heart, so that by his help, they might win souls for him and many might be brought into the fold.'

(Unreferenced newspaper clipping in the *Minutes of the Oxfordshire and East Gloucestershire Baptist Association*, Annual Meetings, 19th-20th May 1931, pp. 145-147).

Appendix 3

Gates placed a written version of her own presidential address in the 1931 *Annual Report* of the Oxfordshire and East Gloucestershire Baptist Association (pp. 1-2).

'President's message

'The attitude of Christ to the nation

'Dear Fellow-workers,

'In dealing with this subject it brings in every individual, because after all nations are comprised of individuals. The League of Nations is a great thing, but not a new thing; 760 years B.C. the nations had the same idea, that there should be no more war, but how is it to be accomplished? Only in so far that the Spirit of Christ is shown. The attitude of Christ to the nation was prophesied 712 years BC. I read "He shall startle many nations", and has He not done this? In His earthly life He was constantly startling those about Him. There was something pretentious, volcanic about Him. He startled people at the time of His birth and up to the time of His death and glorious resurrection.

'1st – *By His Methods.* - Instead of coming amid pageantry and state, He came as the meek and lowly Jesus born in a manger, in a stable. The Jewish conception of the Messiah was that He would make deliverance by conquest, but Christ's conception was by sacrificial and dying love on the cross. He startled the nation by His resurrection, and by asking a woman to proclaim the message 'the Lord is risen'. That was Christ's method.

'2nd – *He was startling in his speech.* - The comment of the people was 'Never man spake like this man.' His speech staggered the Scribes, Pharisees. He told them plainly, God did not want sacrifices so much as He wanted obedience. Think of His teaching on the great doctrine of love. Thou shalt love thy neighbour as thyself. Think of the parable of the Good Samaritan. Work it out. Think of the moral of the story, and He says, 'Go thou and do likewise.' If it was translated into everyday life our nation would be better. If He came personally into our churches to-day I think a good many would be startled. Ministers, deacons, and members need to search their own hearts, as He would search them.

'3rd - *He startled the nation by his deeds.* - Not only by healing the sick, and raising the dead to life, but by reclaiming lost souls. There is no sensation in the world like the rebirth of a soul, to see men and women turn from the power of Satan unto God, and He has left a plan for you and I to carry out, to try and win lost ones back to Him. Too many are at ease in Zion. It is the King's business, and the King's business requireth haste. Let us put away doubts and fears and get a fresh grip on this Mighty Christ, who can startle all the world by His deeds of redeeming grace. This is the Christ whom we preach. The Christ in whom is infinite resources of power. His promise is, Lo, I am with you alway. He will not fail us. Let us then be strong and of good courage, I am with thee saith the Lord.

'Yours in his service

'Edith Gates'

Appendix 4

Baptist Union of Great Britain Minutes 1925-26

Meeting of the BU Council, 9 to 10th February 1926 (Page 789 ff.)

[Item] XII Report of committee re. admission of women to the Baptist Ministry

(a) This committee met on 14 September 1925 and submitted the following statement for consideration: –

It appears that the names of certain women ministers have been placed upon the Accredited List of ministers as given in the Baptist Handbook without helpful discussion either in the Council or in the Assembly. The Committee holds that a novel departure, involving many and large questions, should be the subject of careful consideration by the council and steps taken to regularise the position and to determine upon what conditions, if any, women may be admitted to our list and to any privileges and benefits, such as sustentation or superannuation, that might attach thereto.

The Committee is clear that it would be contrary to Baptist belief and practice to make sex a bar to any kind of Christian service. The church is within its rights in calling a woman to the pastoral or any other office, and this carries with it the right to accept such a call. The principle of the admission of women to the Baptist ministry would, in the opinion of the Committee, be generally approved; the matter in question, however, is their admission to the accredited list.

The Accredited Lists are no more than an expedient; they are required for the proper working of the denominational machine. Omission from it does not involve a judgement on the validity of a particular ministry; it means no more than that it is not valid to qualify for the Benefits to which the Lists admit. The question of the inclusion of women on the Lists is, therefore, solely one of expediency.

It is from this purely practical point of view that the Committee submits the following considerations: –

1. At the present time our Churches are making hardly any demand for women as pasters. Three names only are at present in our lists. They are those of: –

    (i) Mrs Maria Living Taylor, BA who was admitted to the Ministerial List after passing the Baptist Union Examinations and after receiving the usual recommendation from the Essex Association based on two years of efficient pastoral work. She is a colleague with her husband in the pastorate of Sion Jubilee Church, Bradford. She receives no grant from the Sustentation Fund.

    (ii) Miss Edith Gates, Probationer, Baptist Union Examination, who has been minister at Little Tew and Cleveley since 1918, and was recommended by the Oxfordshire Association. Miss Gates receives £33 per annum from the Sustentation Fund.

    (iii) Miss Violet Hedger BD whose name was placed on the Probationers' List on the usual certificate that she had completed a full course at Regent's Park College to the satisfaction of the tutors and committee. The general superintendents did everything in their power to help her by introductions to the churches, but, in spite of her considerable qualifications, Miss Hedger was for a long time without an invitation to the ministry of a Church. (It was explained that since the above paragraph was drawn up, Miss Hedger had accepted a call to Littleover, near Derby, and was in receipt of a grant from the Sustentation Fund.)

(Note. (a) The Committee feels that, in view of the reluctance of our Churches to invite women to the pastorate, the Council should appeal to all College Principals and Committees to make it as clear as possible to all women candidates for the ministry, before admitting them for training, that the prospect of finding such spheres of service as they desire at the end of their College courses is exceedingly small.

(b). In this connection the Committee considered the difficulty created by the fact that at present the denomination accepts students for the Probationers' List on their leaving college, and the consequent obligation to help them find pastorates, although it has no direct voice in the question whether they shall be admitted to College for training, or in the sort of training to be given. It was suggested that this might be a fit subject for discussion by the United Collegiate Board.)

2. The committee considers that, in the raising of the Sustentation Fund, only a ministry of men was contemplated and that some of the provisions of the Trust, which refers specifically only to the cases of married men and unmarried men, prima facie rule women out of its benefits. It therefore recommends that the Honorary Solicitor to the Baptist Union be consulted as to the legality of payments from the sustentation fund to women pastors. In the event of legal opinion being adverse, the admission of women to the Accredited Lists would seem to involve either an alteration of the Trust or entirely separate arrangements for the Sustentation and Superannuation of women ministers.

3. In the event of the council sanctioning the admission of
    women to the accredited lists, the committee is strongly of
    the opinion that it is impolitic to admit married women
    other than widows. Otherwise there would be nothing to
    prevent any minister's wife who is accepted by the church
    as her husband's colleague, conforming to the regulations
    for recognition and being passed on to the lists. In the
    event of her husband's death and the church no longer
    requiring her services she would then seem to become a
    charge on the Sustentation Fund as an unsettled minister.
    Moreover there would be no reason why the wife of a
    layman in secular employment might not similarly qualify
    and situations might be created and very considerable
    embarrassment.

In existing circumstances the Committee is not in a position to
recommend the admission of women to the Accredited Lists.
Having regard, however, to the agreed principle of the rights
of women to admission to the ministry, the Committee invites
the council to consider –

> (i) whether they are prepared to take such steps as shall
> give full effect to the principle by the formation of an
> Accredited List for women with its appropriate
> conditions and benefits; or

> (ii) whether, for the present, the discretionary powers,
> vested in the Council acting through the Ministerial
> Recognition and Homework Fund Committees, shall
> suffice to deal with cases as they arise with such names
> of women as may be approved to be entered on a
> separate list to be entitled 'List of Women Pastors' and
> appearing in the Baptist handbook. To avoid ambiguity
> in the interpretation of the Sustentation Fund Trust the
> heading on the Part III of the Handbook would be

amended to read 'The Accredited list of Baptist
Ministers and Probationers in the British Isles."

*[End of the special statement prepared by the secretary of the original
committee, M. E. Aubrey, and agreed on the 14th September 1925 by
the committee on the Admission of Women to the Baptist Ministry.]*

(b) With reference to paragraph 2 in which it was recommended that
the solicitor to the Baptist union should be consulted as to the legality
of payments from the Sustentation Fund to women pastors, the
following letter, dated 6th October, 1925, was read from Mr Cecil B.
Rooke:–

> With regard to the legal point raised, I am of opinion that if a
> woman's name is placed on one or other of the Ministerial lists
> any payment to her from the Sustentation Fund is perfectly
> valid.
>
> The essential qualification for benefits under the Fund is being
> an 'accredited minister' and the definition of that in the Trust
> Deed is a minister or probationer whose name appears in the
> current edition of the Baptist handbook.
>
> As to the propriety of placing women's names on the
> accredited lists, different considerations apply and it is quite
> obvious that the rules were framed with male candidates only
> in view and I think it will be quite competent for the
> Ministerial Recognition Committee to refuse to recognise
> women as coming under the rules without a resolution from
> the Assembly to the country.
>
> This, however, does not affect the main point, namely, that if a
> woman's name is in fact on the current list she is clearly
> within the benefit of the Sustentation Fund.

(c) Considerable difficulty was felt in respect to the peculiar relation
of women to the Sustentation Fund and the Superannuation Fund, but
after a lengthy discussion it was resolved to adopt the suggestions in

paragraph 3, (i) and (ii) of an accredited list of women pastors with its appropriate conditions and benefits, and that a Committee be appointed to take into consideration the framing of rules under which help could be given under the two Funds named to women whose names appear on the list of women pasters. It was further agreed that the committee be appointed jointly by the executive of the Sustentation Fund and of the Superannuation Fund Committee.

Appendix 5

Edith Gates' obituary

Unattributed, *The Baptist Union Handbook*, 1963, p. 362

GATES, EDITH, was born on 22nd March 1883. Miss Gates felt called to the Christian ministry and in 1918 was invited to the pastorate of the Little Tew and Cleveley Baptist Church. This was at a time when women were not generally regarded as being capable of leadership in religious or secular societies. Edith Gates was one of the first women to pass the Baptist union ministerial examinations and have her name placed on the list of women pastors. For thirty-two years she led the fellowship at Little Tew and Cleveley; she was greatly respected both in the church and in the neighbourhood. On her retirement in 1950 she settled in Weston-Super-Mare. In her will she bequeathed the residue of her estate for religious purposes, including the Superannuation Fund of the Baptist Union and in addition left a specific legacy to the Baptist Homework Fund. Edith Gates died on the 19th January 1962. She was president of the Oxfordshire and East Gloucestershire Association in 1931, and the founder of the Women's Prayer Circle. Many mourn the loss of this gracious Christian lady.

Bibliography

Primary Sources

Baptist Union of Great Britain and Ireland Minute Books

Belmont Baptist Chapel Sunday School Minute Book, Surrey History Centre, 3470/1/1

Clarence Park Baptist Church, Weston-Super-Mare, *Deacons' Minutes*

Clarence Park Baptist Church, *Church Meeting Minutes*

Clarence Park Baptist Church, *Baptist Women's League, Record of Meetings*

Clarence Park Baptist Church, *Minutes of the Baptist Women's League Executive Committee*

Clarence Park Baptist Church, *Monthly Newsletters*

Communion Register, Belmont Free Church, Interdenominational Mission, Item 3470/2/1, Surrey History Centre, Woking

Dancey, Miss Hilda M., letter to Mr W. Carpenter, 9th Jan. 1983; in the possession of Tony Woolfenden of Sutton

Dunkley, Sylvia, *Women Magistrates, Ministers and Municipal Councillors in the West-Riding of Yorkshire, 1918–1939* (Submitted for the Degree of Doctor of Philosophy, Department of History, University of Sheffield, August 1991)

Electoral Register of Lodgers, Sutton, 1911, D. 952

Epsom Baptist Church, minute of members meeting (extracts)

Green, Ray, interviews Weston-Super-Mare, 28.7. 2020 and 28.11.2021

Hamilton, C., *A Pageant of Great Women* (London: The Suffrage Shop, 1910)

London Society for Women's Suffrage Annual Reports

Minutes of the Oxfordshire (and East Gloucestershire) Baptist Association Committee

New Road Baptist Church [Oxford], *Church Book,* Membership List

Ordnance Survey, Surrey, sheet XIX.3 (Banstead; Carshalton; Sutton and Cheam, 1913)

Oxfordshire Baptist Association, Annual Reports

Oxfordshire and East Gloucestershire Baptist Association Minutes

Ray Green, interviews, Weston-Super-Mare, July 2020

St John the Baptist Belmont, Parish Magazine, 1908-1012

The Baptist Union Handbook (Directory)

The National Register, 1939

The Oxford and District Free Church Magazine

The English Church Union and the Lambeth Conference, *The Report of the Committee of the Council, 18th March, 1931* (London: English Church Union)

Women's Prayer Circle Minutes (1931-1950)

Newspapers

Baptist Times and Freeman

Banbury Advertiser

Banbury Guardian

Beckenham Journal

Buckinghamshire Examiner

Bucks Herald

Bury Free Press

Cheltenham Chronicle

Eastbourne Gazette

North Devon Journal

Norwood News

Nottingham Evening Post

Nottingham Journal

Oxfordshire Weekly News

Portsmouth Evening News

The Vote

Uxbridge & W. Drayton Gazette

Wells Journal

Books and articles

Aubrey, M.E., *The Baptist Who's Who: An Authoritative Reference Work and Guide to the Careers of Ministers and Lay Officials of the Baptist Churches* (London: Shaw Publ., 1934).

Bowers, Faith, *A Bold Experiment* (London: Bloomsbury Central Baptist Church, 1999).

Bradley, Katherine, *Faith, perseverance and patience: the history of the Oxford suffrage and anti-suffrage movements, 1870-1930* (Oxford Brookes University, 1997).

Breed, G., ed., *The Baptist Almanack, 1886-1914 [Excluding 1890, 1892, 1896, 1904]: London and Suburban Baptist Directory, Churches Without Pastors, and Ministers Without Churches, Baptist Provincial Directory, Lancashire Baptist Churches, and [From 1905 Onwards], Provincial Baptist Ministers Who Are Settled Pastors, Whose Names Are Omitted From the "List of Baptist Ministers" in the Baptist Handbook; Extracted and Photocopied by Geoffrey R. Breed* (Gillingham: G.R. Breed, 2001).

Chadwick, Rosie, ed., *A Protestant Catholic Church of Christ: Essays on the History and Life of New Road Baptist Church, Oxford* (Oxford: New Road Baptist Church, 2003).

Collis, Michael J. (2014) 'Female Baptist Preachers and Ministers in Wales', *Baptist Quarterly*, 45:8, 465-484.

Craig, C. Leslie, *Splendid the Heritage: the story of Belmont and its Methodist Church* (Craig, 1965).

Gouldbourne, Ruth M.B., *Reinventing the Wheel: Women and Ministry in English Baptist Life*, The Whitley Lecture, 1997-1998 (Oxford: Whitley Publns, 1997).

Green, Ray, *Christ's People at Clarence Park 1900-2000* (Weston-Super-Mare: Ray Green, 2000).

Green, Ray, *More about Christ's People at Clarence Park, Supplement to Centenary Church History of Clarence Park Baptist Church Weston-Super-Mare* (Weston-Super-Mare: Ray Green, 2008).

Hambleton, Michael G., *A Sweet and Hopeful People: The Story of Abingdon Baptist Church, 1649-2000* (Abingdon: Abingdon Baptist Church, 2000).

Lewis, C. S., *Collected Letters vol. 2* (London: HarperCollins, 2004).

Northcroft, D. M., *Free Church Women Ministers* (London: Edgar G. Dunstan, 1930).

Randall, Ian, *The English Baptists of the 20th Century* (Didcot: Baptist Historical Society, 2005).

Reed, Margaret, *A Village Church: the story of the first 75 years of St John's with Belmont Methodists* (Reed, 1992).

Shepherd, Peter, (1999), *John Howard Shakespeare and the English Baptists, 1898-1924*, Durham theses, Durham University. http://etheses.dur.ac.uk/4513/ [Accessed Sept 2022].

Sparkes, Douglas C., *An Accredited Ministry* (Didcot: Baptist Historical Society, 1996).

Sparkes, Roland, *Belmont: A Century Ago, A description of the Belmont area as it existed in 1865* (Belmont and South Cheam Residents' Association, December 2009).

Stockwell, A. H., *The Baptist Churches of Surrey* (London: Arthur H. Stockwell, ND [1909]).

Troughton, Patricia Jean, *Women in Ordained Baptist Ministry: An Investigation of Some of the Factors That Inhibit the Ordained Ministry of Women in Baptist Ministry: With Special Reference to East Anglia* (Cambridge: Cambridge Theological Federation, 2004).

Whitley, W.T., *The Baptists of London* (London: Kingsgate P., [N.D.]).

Woolfenden, Tony, *A Church for Belmont; St John's, its history and a guide* (Belmont Surrey: St John's Church, 2015).

Conference Papers

Rooke, Deborah, 'Violet Hedger', paper given at the CBS Day Conference entitled Bap*tist Women Through the Centuries Marking the Centenery of Violet Hedger's Admission to Ministerial Training* on 30 October 2029 at Regent's Park College, Oxford.

archives.libraries.london.ac.uk/resources/graduates2ocr.pdf [accessed

Websites

archives.libraries.london.ac.uk/resources/graduates2ocr.pdf [accessed Sept. 2022].

Baggs, A. P., Christina Colvin, H. M. Colvin, Janet Cooper, C. J. Day, Nesta Selwyn and A Tomkinson, 'Parishes: Little Tew', in *A History of the County of Oxford: Volume 11, Wootton Hundred (Northern Part)*, ed. Alan Crossley (London, 1983) 247-258. *British History Online* www.british-history.ac.uk/vch/oxon/vol11/pp247-258 [Accessed July 2022].

Belmont and South Cheam Residents Association: www.bscra.com/History.html [accessed Oct. 2022].

Edith Streets: http://edithsstreets.blogspot.com/2017/05/belmont.html [Accessed July 2022].

Little Tew: www.littletew.org.uk [Accessed July 2022].

Oxfordshire Archaeological Unit Newsletter No 1, January 1978, Parish Survey Meeting, 27th November 1977, p. 1, https://library.thehumanjourney.net/296/1/NewsletterOAUJan 1978No.1.pdfA.pdf [Accessed Sept. 2022].

Pisgah Baptist Church: www.pisgah.org.uk/annie-lodwock [Accessed Oct. 2022].

Price, Francis, *A History of Little Tew.* www.littletew.org.uk [Accessed Sept. 2022].

Printed in Great Britain
by Amazon